FROM FREUD TO KAFKA

FROM FREUD TO KAFKA
The Paradoxical Foundation
of the Life-and-Death Instinct

Philippe Réfabert

Translated by Agnès Jacob

KARNAC

First published in French as *De Freud à Kafka* by les Editions Calmann-Lévy

First published in English in 2014 by
Karnac Books Ltd
118 Finchley Road
London NW3 5HT

The following are reproduced with the kind permission of the publisher:

Excerpt from "Sprich auch du" by Paul Celan © CVA, Random House, Munich.

Excerpt from "Encart" in *Le Nu perdu* (1964–1970) © Editions Gallimard, 1971.

British Library Cataloguing in Publication Data

A C.I.P. for this book is available from the British Library

ISBN-13: 978-1-78220-129-8

Typeset by V Publishing Solutions Pvt Ltd., Chennai, India

Printed in Great Britain

www.karnacbooks.com

The roads that do not promise the country of their destination are the best loved.

—René Char, "Encart", *Le Nu Perdu
et autres poèmes* (1966)

CONTENTS

ACKNOWLEDGEMENTS

This book owes its existence to all those whose confidence allowed me to witness the energy they drew from their secret pain, their silent rage, and their hidden wounds. The book is above all a response to their appeal for assistance. Thanks to them, the apprentice I was had to invent analytic strategies making it possible to leave the shores where Sirens sing the praises of conventional thought and voluntary servitude.

ABOUT THE AUTHOR

Philippe Réfabert was born in 1933; he obtained his medical degree in 1962. After working as an in-house doctor in psychiatric hospitals between 1962 and 1966, he set up in private practice as a psychoanalyst in 1967; the practice is currently ongoing.

Between 1963 and 1973, he was a member of the Paris Psychoanalytic Society, where he received training. Subsequently, he became a member of the College of Psychoanalysts and, finally, of the Fédération des Ateliers de Psychanalyse. He served as its president between 1991 and 1992.

Philippe Réfabert is a prolific author, known for his work on the first years of the psychoanalytic movement, and particularly on Freud's relationship with Fliess, with Jung, and with Ferenczi. He conducted a series of seminars on this subject between 1978 and 1985, with Madame Barbro Sylwan.The book *Freud, Fliess, Ferenczi*, published by Hermann in 2010, contains their collected articles.

Between 1986 and 2002, Philippe Réfabert led a seminar on psychoanalytic practice and epistemology. *Epistolettres*, the publication of the "Ateliers", published many of his articles on analytic commitment, on memory and forgetting, and on analytic procedure. The journal of the College of Psychoanalysts, *Psychanalystes*, published "Donner le temps, assurer la couverture" ("Giving time, providing protection"), in 1994 (n° 44). It had also published "Une matrice psychique transitionnelle" ("A transitional psychic matrix") in 1993 (n° 41). "Relire Schreber: proposition pour penser le négativisme" ("Rereading Schreber: an approach to reflecting on negativism") appeared in *Revue Internationale de Psychopathologie*, 1994, n° 15 (P.U.F., Paris). The journal *Pratiques, Les cahiers de la médecine utopique* published "La crise, entre mémoire et oubli" ("Crisis: between remembering and forgetting"), "Le meurtre d'aâme" ("Soul murder"), "Le sexe au service de l'irreprésentable" ("Sex in the service of the unrepresentable") and "Pirandello analyste" ("Pirandello as analyst"), between 1996 and 1999.

Philippe Réfabert participated in the preparation of the book *Les travaux d'Oedipe* ("*The Labours of Oedipus*") (L'Harmattan, Paris, 1994), both as author and editor.

His article "Le témoin, sujet de la psychanalyse" ("The witness, psychoanalysis subject") appeared in *Le Coq-Héron*, Erès, 2002. His most recent articles, "Fliess–Freud, un transfert psychotique" ("Fliess-Freud: a psychotic transference") and "Le témoignage dans la cure" ("Bearing witness in analysis"), appeared in *Epistolettres*, March and April 2003. He contributed the chapter "La théorie de l'hystérie grevée par la carence d'un témoin" (The theory of hysteria in the face of the lacking witness) to the work, *Témoignage et trauma*, edited by Jean-François Chiantaretto, published by Dunod.

Since 2002, Philippe Réfabert has led a workshop on the theme of "Giving time". He is preparing a book on this primal paradoxical endowment. In this endeavour, he makes use of his clinical experience, and of the light and shadow found in the works of poets like Fernando Pessoa and Paul Celan.

PART I

CHAPTER ONE

A misunderstanding between Freud and the man from the country

One means that Evil has is the dialogue.

—Franz Kafka, *"The Third Notebook"* (1917)

Tired of sitting on a stool and counting the lice in the gatekeeper's fur coat while waiting to be admitted to the law, the man from the country went to see a psychoanalyst.

At the start of his psychoanalysis, he was very enthusiastic. The analyst found that his dreams had meaning, and his interpretation of them seemed irrefutable. The man was particularly grateful for these interpretations since they admitted him into a brotherhood where everyone seemed to know what was meant when notions like "the unconscious" or phrases like "the desire to kill the father" were used. He had to admit that, in truth, his inhibitions were related to a repressed desire to penetrate his mother. The incestuous desires he shared with Oedipus were so powerful that they paralysed him. In addition, he lived in fear of reprisal from his father, a formidable rival after all. In short, the man from the country dreaded the consequences of his desire.

But things soon took a strange turn on the couch: he fell asleep. One day, he told his analyst that the words the latter spoke did not enter his ears. This statement had serious repercussions. He learned that the Oedipus complex could be reversed and that he himself was a case in point. His problem took on a completely different meaning—the reverse meaning, in fact. What he wanted was to be penetrated by his analyst, and his inability to enter the law was related, he must understand, to his desire to be penetrated by his father. He accepted these explanations, which seemed valid. He was amazed to see that his analyst could solve all problems by using the notion of the Oedipus complex and of psychic bisexuality. This combination was a master key that could unlock all the mysteries of the unconscious. On the couch, he slept more and more. One day, he awoke with the sensation of having female sex organs. He spoke of this sensation right away, seeing it as a worthy prize to offer his analyst, an expert on psychic bisexuality. Such was his existence on the couch.

On the outside, he was still sitting on a stool before an open door. To help pass the time, he did what many others had done since Freud: he replaced the stool with an armchair and changed from being one-not-analysed to being an analyst.

Another man from the country, very much like himself, came to see him and put him in such a state that he had to look for another analyst for himself. This second psychoanalysis made him see that his oral sadism was so great that it changed into its opposite and that the resulting masochistic tendency, prematurely fixated, prevented him from being admitted where he wanted to be. This analyst was indulgent and counted on the passage of time to wear down his patient's aggression.

In the meantime, the patient developed an interest in the study of texts. He discovered that Freud had made the ego into a Pandora's box, and that his theoretical child was a perverse polymorph governed by a multitude of unconnected drives: homosexual, sadistic, masochistic, voyeuristic, exhibitionist. His own case, that of the man from the country, was an illustration of uncommon sadism. His studies led him to conclude that those of Freud's disciples who still believed the primary and the primitive to be synonymous could not really help him. He could see that Freud had made man heir to a whole store of drives, all clamouring to be satisfied. This line of reasoning in which ontogenesis reproduced phylogenesis was of no help to him and did nothing to change his position vis-à-vis the law. His reaction to the treatment remained negative.

He decided to see a third analyst. This one used the significant scanning method, in other words, short sessions. No more ready-made interpretations and universal recourse to Oedipus. This time, to his great relief, there was no inflation of meaning. Things followed their course, but after a few months the man from the country was surprised to experience a feeling of melancholy and a growing desire to kill himself. He took refuge in a psychiatric hospital. There, comforted by the walled-in garden and the kindness of the people around him, he was inspired to write a story he called "The Bridge" (1931a), which starts:

> I was stiff and cold, I was a bridge, I lay over a ravine. (…) So I lay and waited; I could only wait. Without falling, no bridge, once constructed, can cease to be a bridge.

One day the bridge heard someone approaching and prepared to hold him up. He promised himself that he would help the person cross over to the other side. But when the "someone" came, he started by prodding the bridge's bushy hair with his stick, and then caused the bridge wild pain by jumping with both feet on the middle of his body. Who could it be, the bridge asked himself?

> "A child, a dream, a wayfarer, a suicide, a destroyer?" He turned around to see who it was. But a bridge to turn around! He had not yet quite turned around when he began to fall, he fell and was torn and pierced by the sharp rocks which had always gazed up at him so peacefully from the rushing water. (Kafka, 1931a, p. 411)

This exercise helped him understand what he would have liked to say to Freud and his disciples. He had wanted to tell them that by locking up the oedipal tragedy in the theory of primal repression, by fencing in the ego, Freud had supposed that the man from the country, and everyone else as well, had the ability to turn himself around. He had supposed that every child naturally inherits the ability to make decisions such as the one which consists of saying "I want to take this into myself, I want to keep that out." He had given the child a self-reflective capacity located somewhere between an "I" which takes in and an ego which feels, an "I" which sees and an ego which is seen. Freud had presupposed self-awareness by turning primal repression into a frame with an opening and a closing. Not only did he give the child a clearly defined ego, but also, right from the start, an "I-ego" in which the "I" not only retreats into the background when the ego is busy feeling pleasure or displeasure, but can also count on the support of the ego in order to act, take the initiative, and cross boundaries.

So this was it! The man from the country finally understood what had bothered him about his first analyst, who interpreted his master's teachings too literally.

In truth, this analyst expected the analysand to testify that everyone could be like Oedipus, able to judge himself, conduct his own trial, and accept his incestuous and parricidal intentions without killing himself or going mad. But the witness, exhausted by the heavy responsibility thrust upon him, kept falling asleep.

When a solitary man suspended over a ravine is a bridge unto himself, he is not equipped to turn around. Like Narcissus, he cannot see his own reflection without the risk of drowning. He has no alternative system that would allow him to place the emphasis on the "I" or the ego alternately without losing substance. And so, the man from the country understood that Narcissus was not self-sufficient by choice but by necessity, and that the myth of a primary Narcissus could have disastrous effects. The man from the country decided to relegate this fictional, self-satisfied, self-reliant character to his positivist philosophy function.

More time passed. One day, the man from the country discovered that contrary to what he had believed, Freud had written that displeasure is not necessarily related to increased tension, nor is pleasure always related to its decrease, but that both pleasure and displeasure are characterised by a sort of excitement which could well be rhythm (Freud, 1920g, p. 160). He remembered a dream he had had.

> (… A) frail, tubercular equestrienne on her swaying mount is driven round and round the ring before an unflagging audience by her pitiless, whip-swinging ringmaster for months on end without interruption, whirling about on the horse's back, blowing kisses, ducking and weaving from the waist, and this act, together with the continuous blare of the band and the roaring of the ventilators, goes on and on and down the endless grey avenues of the future, accompanied by the fade and swell of bursts of applause that are really steam hammers—until a young spectator in the gallery runs down the long flight of steps between the rows, bursts into the ring, and

calls: Halt! through the fanfares of the constantly accommodating orchestra. But given (...) that no one, not even the rider seems to notice that the frantic ride is over ... the young man in the gallery, laying his face on the balustrade and sinking into the closing march as into a heavy dream, weeps without knowing it. (Kafka, 1919, p. 401)

The man from the country concluded that Freud, preoccupied as he was with his sexual discoveries, had not taken the time to ask himself where Oedipus had found the resources necessary to build a self-reflective system in which the "I" and the ego are at the same time separate and inexorably linked, and which made him able to judge himself.

He concluded that Freud did not take into account Oedipus' child-hood at Polybius and Merope, and might have thought that it was in the Corinthian nursery where he was placed that his hero had early sustained exposure to the conditions necessary for developing the paradoxical system of reflection that made him able to turn around. Just as had been the case at the start of physics, at the inception of psychoanalysis, Freud had focused his attention far from the origin. He had supposed that the self-reflection which enables man to see himself, to feel, to think, to mirror his own image, was a natural gift. Where Descartes invoked God to legitimise his "I think", Freud referred to an inherent capacity for judgment and self-reflection.

Things were becoming clear to him. By undergoing psychoanalysis, the man from the country had signed a bill of change with Freud, but he fell into lethargy on the couch when his psychoanalyst, loyal to the master, tried to cash it in. An edict hidden in the foundations had excluded him from the field of psychoanalysis—a field its founder had created within a built-in spatial and temporal fence. And the man from the country kept trying to show his analyst that in his world a merry-go-round kept turning day and night in a field without fences. Therein lay the source of their misunderstanding and their failure to see eye to eye. These psychoanalysts wanted to introduce sense where the man from the country suggested there was no sense, and that this absence of enclosure had nothing to do with sense, unless one wanted to speak of an original flaw in the conditions of sense-making.

Thanks to this misunderstanding, he set up camp on the border of the country to which he was seeking entry. There, encouraged by the trust placed in him by passers-by asking him the way, by what he learned from his successes, and, above all, from his failures, and enlightened by the texts of the illustrious men who had passed on the torch before him, Sandor Ferenczi, Michael Balint, Nicolas Abraham, Jacques Lacan, Donald Winnicott, Harold Searles, Robert Langs, and some others, he undertook to find a path of his own to the founding principles, while contributing to building the "road that walks by itself", to borrow the phrase used by Charles Nicolle to refer to infectious diseases.

CHAPTER TWO

Oedipus' answer to Freud's enigma

The thornbush is the old obstacle in the road. It must catch fire if you want to go further.

—Franz Kafka, "*The Third Notebook*" (1917)

The Oedipus complex is the founding myth of psychoanalysis. Starting with *The Interpretation of Dreams* in 1900, Freud placed it at the centre of a field constructed on terrain conquered from both medicine and religion; he was to maintain the central position of this myth until his death. In fact, he would establish the universality of the principle that every child is a budding Oedipus in fantasy—a principle which defies all theoretical restructuring (1900a, p. 263).[1] Freud sees Oedipus' tragedy as consisting of the reaction to the two typical dreams of incest and parricide he considers constitutive of the human psyche. If Oedipus is taken as a model for every child, psychoanalysis becomes a scientific field, a coherent set of concepts and ideas.

Oedipus first appeared in the correspondence between Freud and Fliess in September 1897 (Masson, 1985, p. 15). Up until then, psychoanalytic technique was being created, symptoms were given meaning, but no theory of normal psychic activity had been elaborated. That year,

Freud made a decisive founding gesture by asserting that the origin of psychic life is not to be found in material or spiritual determinism, but rather in the tension created in the child by language and its ensuing cohort of questions, and most of all questions related to differences between the sexes and between generations.

Maintaining that every child is a budding Oedipus constitutes a break with all materialist perspectives, and especially that of Fliess. The latter, Freud's close friend and confidant, and for many years his only intellectual interlocutor, was convinced that human life is ruled by the rhythms of feminine and masculine cycles (Fliess, 1909, p. 1).[2] Like certain modern neurobiologists, Fliess explained the contingencies of human existence using the hidden laws of matter. It might be that he showed himself to be more rigid and superficial than others regarding these principles; whatever the case, Freud violently rejected this materialist determinism, replacing it with a myth.

In January 1899, when Fliess, puzzled or perhaps annoyed, asked what happens in early childhood, Freud replied: "Nothing." No particular event takes place; rather, the child carries within him a "sexual impulse" which will develop into a life story optimally and universally illustrated by the legend of Oedipus. Possessing language, and especially speech, the child is an inventor of stories. Using the events of his own history, he will write particular variations on the major themes provided by primal fantasies.[3] Thus, at the start, the child is both author and actor in a drama where characters desire each other, exchange words, investigate, condemn each other, and inflict injury or death. To the question of what is there at the origin, Freud replies that a fiction is germinating in the child. Through Oedipus, Freud audaciously intends to found a new scientific field on a fiction.

At the same time, Oedipus allowed Freud to oppose Jung and, beyond him, all spiritual perspectives of psychic life.[4] Jung believed that the forces of good and evil are engaged in a conflict bearing no relation to particular individuals. It is not possible to assign an origin to the unconscious; the *living psyche*, existing since all eternity, manifests itself in human dreams naturally (Jung, 1963, p. 157).[5] This notion is what allows Jung to declare in peremptory fashion that dreams are neither dead content nor second-hand forms of life, but rather the expression of this *psyche* which carries divine and demonic forces. Most of all, this *psyche* takes no account of generational discontinuity, and death is no obstacle to it. When Jung dreams of a knight in twelfth-century armour, he identifies him as a knight of the Holy Grail returning to take up his interrupted quest. Thanks to Jung's dream about the knight, the quest for spirituality, for the "numinous" as he calls it, was going to be taken up again.[6]

Jung disregards discontinuity between generations, as well as between animal and mineral realms. In his view, the spiritual knows no boundary and can manifest itself in the mineral, vegetable, animal, or human realm indifferently. An incident he describes in his autobiography illustrates the relation between these realms. In 1909, in the course of a conversation with Freud, Jung asks the latter for his opinion on parapsychology and foresight. Freud answers that he gives no credence to such phenomena. But, just then, the cupboard starts to squeak; Jung seizes the opportunity to point out that the cupboard is trying to make a point, and tells his doubting interlocutor that the squeaking will be repeated. And sure enough, in a few moments the same noise is heard again (ibid., p. 152).[7] Thus, the *psyche* can manifest itself in a cupboard as well as in a dream: it transcends all realms without distinction.

Jung's views are similar to those held by Fliess, in so far as both men are trying to establish laws applying to the animal and vegetable realms, as well as to the human race. In *The Course of Life*, Fliess points out that plant buds appear at twenty-eight or twenty-three day intervals, and that the number of days it takes for ostrich eggs to hatch is a multiple of twenty-three (1906, p. 252). Jung's laws of the *psyche* and Fliess's laws of matter have the same structure. Both place the destiny of a plant in the same realm as that of a human being. This deprives man of any possibility to change his destiny, since spiritual forces in the first case and material forces in the second make him the possible plaything of immanent powers. What these theories have in common is that they both erase the paradox of human existence which evolves under the sign of discontinuity *and* continuity. When the human and the non-human are governed by the same laws, the human is enticed by the Sirens of science, and invited to forget what sets it apart in the universe: the ability to conceive death, and awareness of the discontinuity between generations.

While Fliess and Jung speak for continuity, Freud advances the coexistence of continuity and discontinuity, both present in the child. Both Fliess and Jung imply that in the human realm something escapes the inscription of death. By contrast, Freud's founding principle: "Every child was once a budding Oedipus" inscribes discontinuity into every birth (Masson, 1985, p. 272).[8] What is there in the beginning? A speaking being confronted with enigmas, a child obliged to answer the questions raised by existence and by the origin of existence. In order to pursue his concept of the particularity of death in the human realm, Freud distanced himself from Fliess and later from Jung, and persisted in believing, against all odds, in his founding fiction based on two major assertions: the child is the place of origin of psychic life, and the name of this child is Oedipus.

But this attempt to define the origin without falling into the materialist or spiritual trap is only partly successful. The choice of Oedipus signals the attempt, but it also leads to its failure. While Oedipus makes it possible for Freud to conceive a new myth of the origins, which inscribes man in the double register of life and death, of continuity and discontinuity, this hero will also lead back to the safe terrain of natural philosophy. Freud sees Oedipus as representing the incestuous posture, a posture Freud takes for granted as natural. This presumption makes the sexual a given, something natural, in short, a substance. Those who follow this doctrine will be inclined to erase the discontinuity between the human and the animal. Therefore, the sexual is the portion of the theory where the continuity-discontinuity paradox encounters a stumbling block.

To understand how the theoretical edifice was constructed on this stumbling block, we have to go back to 1893, the year when Freud's almost exclusive correspondence with Fliess began. That year, Freud declared that all depression is sexual in origin; soon afterwards, he asserted that the sexual is the "pass key" which unlocks the mystery of all psychic suffering. Freud is now convinced that psychic problems are linked to the trauma that early sexual seduction inflicts on the child. But this "trauma theory" is not confirmed in every case, and does not provide Freud with the foundation of a universal theory of psychic process. In September 1897, he makes a drastic decision: he abandons trauma theory and turns to Oedipus, who assures him that seduction is endogenous, inherent to the human condition. Now, the theory is founded on the idea that sexuality is traumatic in itself, and that psychic life develops along the lines of the legend of Oedipus and of the primal fantasies this legend organises. The concept of hysteria founded on early seduction is replaced by the concepts of psychic life in general, and of primary sexuality. This allows Freud to advance that seduction is internal before being external.

Up until 1897, the child was seen as the possible object of a seducer. While the theory placed him in this position, he could only appeal a judgment and, whether or not the appeal was heard, he remained in a passive position. oedipal theory, on the other hand, transforms the child from the passive victim of an assault into the subject and object of psychic disturbances provoked by this assault, seen as internal. The patient becomes the subject of his drama, participates in writing and directing it, and, as a result, can hope to find in himself the resources needed to change the text, the plot, and its outcome. In this conceptual framework, the child, within his means, and later the child in the adult, is responsible for his own destiny. But abandoning trauma theory exposed psychoanalytic theory to the risk of reviving the concept of individual "constitution", that is, the notion of atavistic transmission, prevalent throughout the nineteenth century. The advent of Oedipus amounted to returning to natural philosophy and to the naturalist scientific paradigm which erases the frontier between animal and human. The fact is that if the child harbours, from the beginning, and incestuous and parricidal impulse, the discontinuity Freud had invented to define the human is eliminated. Inborn sexuality, that of Oedipus, that of every child, is the element which brings the entire conceptual edifice into the sphere of immanence, the sphere which encompasses all natural philosophy. When psychoanalysis takes this direction, it loses the singularity of its endeavour—that of unfolding in the space between the psychic and the somatic outside any existing determination, already given and unquestioned.

Notes

1. The notes Freud added in 1914 and in 1919 to his 1900 masterpiece (*The Interpretation of Dreams*) testify to the importance he attributed to this concept, as well as to the vehement opposition it encountered: "None of the findings of psychoanalytic research has provoked such embittered denials, such fierce opposition—or such amusing contortions—on the part of critics as this indication of the childhood impulses towards incest which persists in the unconscious. An attempt has even been made recently to make out, in the face of all experience, that the incest should only be taken as symbolic" (1900a).

   In 1919, Freud went so far as to add that "... the Oedipus complex, which was touched upon for the first time in the above paragraphs in *The Interpretation of Dreams*, throws a light of undreamed of importance on the history of the human race and the evolution of religion and morality" (ibid., p. 263).

2. In *About Life and Death* (*Vom Leben und vom Tod*, 1909, p. 1) Fliess writes: "All life proceeds according to an internal mechanism inherent to the living organism." He had found an arithmetical formula making it possible to predict all important life events by combining twenty-three day masculine cycles with twenty-eight day feminine cycles.

3. Primal fantasies are directly linked to the position of Oedipus, and they all concern the question of the origin. Primal scene fantasies provide answers to the enigma of the origins, seduction fantasies to the origin of sexuality, and castration fantasies to the enigma of the difference between the sexes.

4. To say that in 1900 Freud is reacting to the psychiatrist who will be his favourite disciple between 1909 and 1911 is premature, since Freud would only meet Jung in 1908. However, as is well known by those interested in the beginnings of psychoanalysis, the Oedipus complex only became an accepted principle after 1910, once *Totem and Taboo* (1912–13) was published and the psychoanalytic institution was established. Therefore, it is reasonable to advance that the hypothesis of the Oedipus complex, the central complex of neuroses, opposed not only Fliess's materialism, but also the spiritual determinism passionately advocated by Jung.

5. "I was never able to agree with Freud that the dream is a "façade" behind which its meaning lies hidden [...]. To me dreams are a part of nature, which harbours no intention to deceive [...]. Long before I met Freud I regarded the unconscious [...] as a natural process to which no arbitrariness can be attributed, and above all no legerdemain" (Jung, 1963, p. 157).

6. In this dream, the knight confronts an old "phantom" border guard, carrier of the forces of the past, in whom Jung recognises Freud, who is about to faint.

7. "[...] You are mistaken, Herr Professor. And to prove my point I now predict that in a moment there will be another loud report!" Sure enough, no sooner had I said the words than the same detonation went off in the bookcase [...] Freud only stared aghast at me" (ibid., p. 152).

8. Unless it is budding sexual excitement, as we will see later. For now, Freud's reflection is situated between a materialist view and a religious spiritualist view. Psychoanalysis, Freud's creation in this context, is the monument that testifies to the attempt to free the question of the origin and destiny of the psyche-soma from the spiritualist and materialist trap in which it had fallen. The problem to be solved concerned this freeing, a freeing that remains to be repeatedly renewed.

CHAPTER THREE

A presumed paradoxical endowment

Tragic reversal is truth emptied out and least united.

—Hölderlin, *"Remarks on Oedipus"* (1803)

In *Oedipus Rex*, two opposed action principles confront each other and lead the tragedy to a point of balance where all meaning is abolished (Hölderlin, 1803, pp. 64–72).[1] This balance between "that which holds man in its grip and that which is the object of his interest" is an anti-rhythmic caesura Hölderlin considers characteristic of tragedy. This model also applies to human existence, since "[T]he most dangerous moment in the course of a day [that is, a life] or of a work of art is when the spirit of time *and* of nature [which oppose each other], that which is divine, which holds man in its grip, *and* the object of his interest confront each other in the fiercest manner …"

"That which holds man in its grip" is to be understood as the words that convey his place in the order of generations and of the difference between the sexes. "That which holds man in its grip" is the term which designates a particular place, excluding him from all places not his and leading him to separation. Hölderlin assigns this term to the sphere of the divine. "The object of his interest", refers to that which

15

man "possesses" that is, everything he places under the heading "my parents", "my children", "my property", and which Hölderlin assigns to the sphere of human concerns, of the mundane.

The divine action principle, born of the requirement of speech, and the mundane principle are locked in a combat whose outcome is uncertain. *Oedipus Rex* is moving because it illustrates the human paradox of being subjected to the need for loyalty to two opposing forces. In the course of a lifetime, these two heterogeneous, radically opposed forces are engaged in a struggle that smoulders quietly most of the time. When the struggle bursts into flame, we speak of a crisis. This life crisis is a dramatic event that leaves man in a paradoxical time-space where all representation is abolished, where his destiny hangs in the balance between life and death. Tragedy is the dramatic form which represents this moment.

> The meaning of tragedies can most easily be understood in a paradox. Since all properties are evenly distributed, everything related to the origin appears not in its original form, but rather in its weakness, so that in fact, the clearest light of life illuminates the weakness of the whole. Thus, in a tragedy, the sign itself is insignificant, but the origin is apparent at first sight. (Schaffer, 1983)

According to Hölderlin, what distinguishes tragedy is the presence of a moment whose sign is equal to zero. In this catastrophic moment, time is interrupted and it is impossible to say what course the hero's destiny will take. This caesura that Hölderlin calls anti-rhythmic is a point where the tensions of opposing signs cancel each other out. The caesura marks the height of the crisis, which in *Oedipus Rex* coincides with the moment of revelation. This catastrophe—a turning point—will give rise to a new Oedipus, the one who will travel to Colona.[2]

When Freud makes his reading of *Oedipus Rex* paradigmatic and exclusive, transforming the normal child into the monstrous hero of the legend, the patient is placed in the position of having to purify himself of his original parricidal and incestuous monstrousness. By adopting this view, Freud subscribed to the positivist scientific consensus of his era, and authorised impatient disciples to base their practice on the Broussais therapeutic principles, best symbolised by bloodletting and purging. But, most importantly, Freud made the purely monstrous figure of the mythical hero (see Goux, 1990) coincide with that of the tragic hero, one able to find a solution to a paradoxical situation having no solution in its given frame of reference. The solution is created by entering another frame of reference. Up until now, powerful and respected, Oedipus ruled over the city of Thebes, which he had delivered from pestilence. Now, "divine order", conveyed by the oracle, demands that the city pay a debt owed since the death of Laius. By accepting this debt, Oedipus comes into conflict with his interests as king, his own mundane interests, precipitating the crisis that places his destiny in the balance. At the end of this moment whose sign is equal to zero, Oedipus' destiny continues on its course. He does not kill himself and does not go mad.

Freud tacitly credits Oedipus with the natural faculties of a tragic hero, specifically a hero who can conduct the trial leading to his seeing himself as he is: incestuous and parricidal. Endowed with this image, Freud's hero, and therefore every child, can claim to be able to face the image reflected in the mirror of his own *psyche* without dying, like Narcissus, or attributing the image to a stranger, like the paranoid patient. But what is the origin and the nature of this faculty which allows Oedipus not to confuse his image with what he is, to keep a distance between these two manifestations? To understand the origin of Freud's assumption, we must go back to that moment in the history of psychoanalysis when Oedipus dazzled Freud by providing the perfect answer to a contradiction.

In 1897 when he invented his oedipal theory, Freud was trying to reconcile two contradictory facts. Although all his women patients had confessed to having been sexually seduced, Freud found that not all of their fathers were guilty of incest. This seemingly insoluble dilemma finds an answer in Jocasta's words: "In their dreams, all men have shared their mother's bed and killed their father." This means that all men desire their mothers. But anyone who questions Oedipus risks being dazzled as well as blinded, offended like the female Sphinx was (ibid.).

As soon as Oedipus solved Freud's dilemma, the latter replaced trauma theory with the concept of fantasy. From that moment on and until his death, Freud asked himself how it was that Oedipus the criminal was also the one who could see his own reflection, be his own judge and submit to the sentence he himself pronounced. Where Oedipus found the resources to overturn the figure of the incestuous and parricidal criminal without going mad or killing himself is a question which, in the haste of laying the foundations, was left to fate—that is, relegated to the idea of nature.

The ability to see oneself, to look back at one's image in order to step away from it, is not inborn. Rather, it is linked to the capacity of the maternal environment to encourage the development of a primary paradoxical system in the child. This system in which continuity and discontinuity are linked is the anchor of heterogeneous sequences of "yes" and "no", of the name and the thing, of the container and the content, of the I and the ego (for development of this idea, see Chapter Six). Seduced by his hero's answer, Freud confuses his capacity for reflection with his incestuous and parricidal image. This image leads him to conclude that every child is Oedipus *a minima* in fantasy, and further, that the child is able to create a representation of Oedipus' crimes in his imagination.

But all of these functions are symbolic, that is, they are the end result of a process where elements of conflict between two antagonistic poles are redefined (Abraham & Torok, 1994). The capacity for fantasy and for reflection presupposes a leap, and this leap presupposes solid ground on which to take a run-up; a primary paradoxical system is what provides this ground.[3] A self-image implies that a paradoxical system formed by the trace of death and the objection to death is in place. When this is the case, the subject can experience the presence of a self which sees and an ego which is seen, and can sustain this indivisibility-divisibility without suffering. By adopting Oedipus as a model, Freud acquired access to representation. He left it to his successors to define the conditions necessary to develop the faculty to symbolise.

Finding a solution to a paradoxical situation and being able to symbolise are naturally coexisting capacities. By giving the theoretical child the ability to invent a solution to a tragic situation—when he says that "every child is a budding Oedipus in fantasy", Freud also grants him the ability to represent the absent object in his imagination, to picture it before finding it in reality. Freud calls this "satisfaction experience". But being able to construct a representation of the object of satisfaction indicates that integration of otherness has been achieved, since the child can picture that which is not present. This original gift Freud bestowed on the child has been the source of much misunderstanding—and much clinical fumbling—because, in fact, not every child receives this faculty naturally, given that its development depends on a maternal environment able to nurture it. Those who did not receive this gift must compensate using their own means. They must also accept that help cannot come from a psychoanalyst convinced that the primary ability to integrate with the other is natural. In establishing the foundations of psychoanalysis, Freud asserted the universality of this gift. He made it one of his founding principles, included it among the fundamental precepts on which he built his scientific edifice. This gift is part of the metapsychological foundation, since it helps to define the concepts of instinct, narcissism, and repression. These concepts are the very subject of psychoanalysis: they are literally "that which under-lies" (sub-jectum).

> Let us imagine ourselves in the position of an almost entirely helpless living organism, as yet unorientated in the world and with stimuli impinging on its nervous tissue. The organism will soon become capable of making a first discrimination and a first orientation. On the one hand, it will detect certain stimuli which can be avoided by an action of the muscles (flight): these it ascribes to an outside world—on the other hand, it will also be aware of stimuli against which such action is of no avail and whose urgency is in no way diminished by it—these stimuli are the tokens of an inner world, the proof of instinctual needs. The appreciative substance of the living organism will thus have found in the efficacy of its muscular activity a means[4] for discriminating between "outer" and "inner".
>
> We thus find our first conception of the essential nature of an instinct by considering its main characteristics, its origin in sources of stimulation within the organism and its appearance as a constant force, and thence we deduce one of its further distinguishing features, namely, that no actions of flight avail against it. (Freud, 1917d, pp. 237–258)

When Freud states that in the beginning there are instinctual needs in the body, he separates the origin of instincts from the indivisible link between the body and the psyche. Although "in the beginning" is no doubt meant to have a mythical sense, an oscillating ambiguity between nature and fiction persists. The natural pole of this ambiguity is rooted in the notion of needs, a notion that exerts magical power on the mind of any observer because it appears evident. But this appearance is misleading, because a need is born of the resonance between the biological foundation—which we will define later—and the maternal disposition to interact with it. Basing the definition of instinct on the notion of need constitutes the weak link in the theory, the door left ajar for naturalism to enter. The concept of need, or of instinctual need, forces psychoanalysis to locate itself in the old ontological paradigm in which something is there since the beginning of time, waiting to be named. In this instance, despite himself, Freud steps back into the medical frame of reference.

The concept of instinct implies another notion: that of a boundary between within and without. When the inside of the body is defined in terms of instinctual stimuli, and instinct is defined in terms of the inside of the body, this circularity transforms impulse into a carrier of the value of the limit. This self-defined axiom states that impulse transfers the figure of the limit to the ego, ascribing to it an assumed limit. One of the corollaries to this hypothesis hidden in the foundations is the assumption that the ego is a separate entity whose boundary is not dependent on the relation with the maternal environment. Thus, impulse, which is a psychosomatic concept and as such specifically human, is given a conceptual origin linked to natural philosophy.

The essential role of instinct, and therefore of the sexual, an idea firmly rooted in the discourse of his time, was one that Freud never entirely discarded. In fact, practice has stayed ahead of theory because the concept of the sexual was never fully humanised; it always maintained a link with animal reproductive instinct, preventing dissociation from the animal realm. Dazzled by his discovery of the primacy of the sexual in 1893, Freud was unable to question this conclusion that had made him assert that all neurasthenias have a sexual origin. In the beginning of that year, he wrote to his friend Fliess that he wanted to use clinical observation to confirm that neurasthenia can only be a sexual neurosis. He underlined "only", making the sexual exclusive. Some years later, when the sexual became something budding in the child, it remained exclusive but acquired a new status.

The discovery of Oedipus, a seducer in the bud, changed the status of the sexual from primary to original. To say that something exists at the origin is a philosophical invitation to review the metaphysics of presence. It is to engage in ontological discourse which incorporates the idea of nature and of human constitution, and which exiles the human from history. To assert that in the human realm the sexual is primary is to say that it is not possible to describe non sexual or non sexualised psychosomatic events. But to assert that the sexual is *at the origin* is another matter. To say that human beings are constitutionally endowed with sexual tendencies and impulses is to place them outside history and deprive them of the means to conceive what these tendencies and impulses might symbolise, what dramas they can help humanise through symbolic representation.

But let us go back to the notion of original closure. When Freud developed the notion of narcissism in 1910, even before inventing the concept of instinct, he had already established closure as a fact. His observation of psychotic patients, particularly patients with megalomania, led him to advance the hypothesis that this affection reflects a state common to all children (1914c).[5] Working back from the evidence of this delusional syndrome, Freud inferred the normal and established primary narcissism as a fact. Based on the Broussais principle established by Auguste Comte—a principle which states that the difference between the normal and the pathological is only a matter of degree—he asserts, as he asserted earlier that every child is a "budding Oedipus", that in the beginning every child is autarchic, disposed to find pleasure only in himself, in short, that every child is a budding Narcissus. Primal narcissism becomes one of Freud's basic precepts, just like the concept of a budding Oedipus. Once again, the child harbours the monstrous and only attains humanity when his vital needs force him to make concessions. From the start, the child, a budding Narcissus just as he is a budding Oedipus, is given a natural limit, an inborn closure.

The review of the theory in 1920 did not change this principle of presumed closure, but it modified its terms. The original ego was no longer seen as a huge ego that eventually reduces its pretensions; rather it was seen as containing, from the beginning, erotic impulses presumed to be unifying, and destructive impulses presumed to play a separating role.

This new perspective views autism as a sign of withdrawal of primary libidinal impulses, and no longer as a resurgence of the original autarchic ego. The negativity of certain psychiatric patients becomes the sign of a withdrawal of libidinal components, which leaves the field open to destructive impulses and to denial. But, once again, the child is endowed with closure.

The notion of closure was to find its most explicit form in the idea of repression, which completes the conceptual framework on which Freud built his theory. Repression is the fundamental defence mechanism Freud saw at work in all psychic illnesses, before he assigned it specifically to hysteria. In 1915 he visualised the following scene to illustrate secondary repression. A visitor enters the hall of a house before attempting to penetrate into the living room. This unwelcome visitor, who has bad intentions, would break the door open if a guard was not there to stop him (1915d).[6] In this scene, the house represents the dwelling place of the ego. The fact that it is locked and protected by a guard is what interests us here.[7]

Thus, Freud endows the child with inborn closure. This property, characteristic of impulses, primary narcissism, and repression, explains the fact that metapsychology and transfer theory have never coexisted smoothly. In fact, if the origin of instinct and narcissism is placed in the natural sphere, while transfer has its origin in the relation between two human beings, the interface between nature and humanity cannot be conceptualised. If Oedipus is another name for instinct, he is placed outside the sphere of the relational, since discontinuity is one of his inherent attributes. From this closed place granted him from the beginning, the child is assumed to be able to judge what is good or bad for him, as well as whether a thing is located in reality or not. The ability to determine the reality of a thing is also presumed as a matter of fact (1925h). The psychoanalyst who removed this epistemological obstacle created the conditions necessary to conduct the treatment of the man from the country.

Notes

1. Hölderlin was the first to describe this struggle in his "Remarks on the Translation of Sophocles", a text essential to my reflection. I am indebted to P. Lacoue-Labarthe for his comments on this text, in *La Fiction du Politique* (1987, pp. 64–72).
2. René Thom's reference to a point of "turning back" (1975) is well-suited to represent the figure of catastrophe.
3. This paradoxical system will be described in Chapter Six, but we can define it here as being constituted by the inscription of the trace of death in life, established in the normal parent–child couple by the combined movements of absorption and expulsion.
4. Emphasis added (in German: *Anhaltspunkt*).
5. "[…] megalomania itself is no new creation; on the contrary, it is, as we know, a magnification and plainer manifestation of a condition which had already existed previously" Freud (1914c, p. 75).

6. "I must set a permanent guard over the door which I have forbidden this guest to enter, since he would otherwise burst it open" (Freud, 1915d).

7. Closure is reinforced by the notion of primal repression, consisting in the psychical representative of the instinct "being denied entrance into the conscious". Here, a psychic representative originally produces its own erasure. Primal repression is the exception which establishes repression, just as the typical dream is the exception which confirms dream mechanisms. Here, the psychic representative of the repressed impulse brings about its own negation and becomes fixed. To the natural closure of a self-defined impulse is added the closure of the primal repression principle that connects pressure and counter-pressure.

CHAPTER FOUR

Sketches of the paradoxical system in Freud's work

> He asked me several things, but I couldn't answer, indeed I didn't even understand his questions. So I said: "Perhaps you are sorry now that you invited me, so I better go" and I was about to get up. But he stretched his hand out over the table and pressed me down: "Stay," he said, "that was only a test. He who does not answer the questions has passed the test."
>
> —Franz Kafka, "The Test", 1936b

In "A Project for a Scientific Psychology" (not published until 1950), in the very early stages of his research, in order to formulate a description of mental functioning, Freud imagined a mechanism characterised by two tendencies: the tendency to discharge and the tendency to restraint. Is this a paradoxical system? Not quite, since in such a system two heterogeneous elements are tied together by a copula. When we speak of *the* tendency to discharge and of *the* tendency to restraint, we dissociate the two components, which can enter into conflict but which do not form a paradoxical system. Such a polarity forms a paradoxical system when the tendency to discharge is inseparable from the tendency to restraint, when one cannot be described without the other.

25

The system is then characterised by the tendency to discharge *and* to restraint, and can justifiably be called paradoxical.[1]

Five years after writing the *Project*, in *The Interpretation of Dreams* (1900a), Freud presents the concept of the pleasure principle, which he sees as governing the psychic apparatus with its three phases: the unconscious, the preconscious, and consciousness. According to this first hypothesis borrowed from Epicurus and Lucretius, unpleasure is linked to an accumulation of tension that the psychic apparatus attempts to evacuate. This impulse to discharge, called desire, leads to investment of the memory of the object of satisfaction. If not impeded, the impulse to discharge leads to hallucinatory satisfaction. Thus, given free rein, desire would lead this "early psychic apparatus" to exhaustion. In order to compensate for this spontaneous tendency to extinction, and to account for the perpetuity of the apparatus, Freud had to conceive of a second system serving to inhibit the system governed by the pleasure principle.[2]

Thus, he describes a first system compatible with the pleasure principle—a system of primary processes, and a second system that, by inhibiting primary process, leads to the satisfaction of needs. This second system is governed by secondary processes.[3] The two systems are described as functioning in parallel, and do not constitute a paradoxical system.

At the same time, Freud describes two types of instincts: ego instincts or instincts of self-preservation, and sexual instincts. Phenomena related to ego instincts are modified in the course of psychic development and, through vital necessity, must submit to the reality principle characterising the secondary system. In contrast, sexual instincts are isolated from all other instincts and left to be governed by the primary system. Thus, the sexual impulse is excluded from the paradoxical design that Freud never stopped seeing as a possibility.

The psychical representatives of sexual impulses in children remain under the rule of the primary system: that is, they are governed solely by the pleasure principle. They are repressed during latency and emerge subsequently in response to premature solicitation, or in adolescence. The person is then defenceless, since he is subjected to a kind of seduction from within. In this progression, sexual instincts, unlike any of the others, remain governed by primary processes only.[4]

The separation of sexual instincts from the other wishful impulses is implicitly posited as an axiom. Sexual instincts are excluded from the other instinctual forces that are not required for "survival". These forces remain unchanged because they do not influence vital phenomena which, in order to endure, must submit to secondary processes and to the inhibition of immediate satisfaction.

The semantic slide from primary to primal is what allowed Freud to posit as inalterable the location of sexual impulses in the primary phase constituting the unconscious. In fact, very early in his work he states that primacy also means first in a time sequence, and that the primary process is present from the start, while secondary processes develop gradually in the course of psychic life. Speaking of the primary, Freud explains that it refers not only to a topographic hierarchy and to function, but also to time relations; in fact, he continues, he intended to say primal as much as primary. Thus, the primary is not merely a topographic indication, but also a historical one. Because the emergence of secondary processes is spaced out over time, the double background of our psychic apparatus is apparently made up of wishful impulses that have escaped the attacks and inhibitions of the preconscious. The representations of infantile sexual impulses remain absent from preconscious thoughts and escape the inhibition of secondary processes. These thoughts or memories are left alone, exempt all along from supervision by the preconscious.[5]

Before 1919, Freud developed a dualistic theory comprised of two tendencies (a tendency to discharge and a tendency to restraint), two processes (a primary one which is also primal, and a secondary one emerging subsequently), and two types of wishful impulses or instincts: the sexual, and all the others. Only self-preservation instincts, which will become the ego instincts, enter into the construction of a paradoxical system.

This conceptual framework remains rooted in naturalistic philosophy because it implies that ego instincts are present from the start, along with sexual instincts. And there is more. The positivist aspect embedded in the foundations of psychoanalysis is evident in the assertion that the psychic apparatus is characterised by the primal modes of functioning associated with natural phenomena.

"A Note upon the 'Mystic Writing-Pad'" (1925a) and *Beyond the Pleasure Principle* (1920g) are the two works in which Freud comes closest to a paradoxical model associating continuity and discontinuity. In these texts, Freud sets aside a conception based on two systems, primary and secondary, and places the description of a psychic apparatus, on which he has been working for thirty years, in a new framework. This new model illustrates the double, contradictory function of the psychic apparatus, which must register permanent traces of the stimuli received while at the same time acting as a clean sheet for new stimuli. "The mystic writing-pad is the model for an apparatus which allows Freud to relegate to a storage room all auxiliary apparatus he had imagined, and particularly optical devices" (Derrida, 1978, p. 224).[6]

On the mystic writing-pad, the writing vanishes as soon as the close contact between the paper receiving the stimulus and the wax slab that preserves the writing is brought to an end. Freud supposed that in the psychic apparatus things proceed as if the unconscious possessed periodic excitability and sent the perception-consciousness system a discontinuous current of stimuli that might constitute the origin of the concept of time.[7]

In order to illustrate an apparatus that stores mnemetic traces and, at the same time, remains a clean sheet receptive to new inscriptions, Freud uses the analogy of a mystic writing-pad on which one hand inscribes the traces while the other periodically lifts up the celluloid sheet: the receptive surface. Jacques Derrida observes that this alternation of excitation and erasure is what creates the space of writing. The inscription-erasure system relies on the support of the inscription and actualises it as well.[8] This is indeed a paradoxical system, but Freud would later bury it in the notion of the unconscious.

Freud maintains that perception and consciousness are connected to a current of innervation sent out periodically by the unconscious. He supposes that cathectic innervations are sent from within in rapid periodic impulses into the preconscious system, and are then withdrawn from it. According to Freud, it is as if, through the preconscious system, the unconscious sent out feelers towards the external world. By introducing the concept of a current of innervation, cathectic innervation (*Besetzunginnervation*) coming from the unconscious, Freud substantiates the "unconscious" and goes back to the reasoning which had made him place the origin of instinct in the body: he returns to the paradigm of presence. This lets us suppose that when Freud discusses the origin he departs from the notion of separate systems and is seduced by ontological reasoning; but, just as Newton had done in his *Principia*, Freud buried the intuition of a paradoxical system in the principles he elaborated.

The clearest expression of a paradoxical system is to be found in *Beyond the Pleasure Principle*, written in 1919. Here, Freud goes so far as to conceive of a single instinct, the death instinct. Starting with the idea that the aim of instinct is to restore an earlier state, Freud takes the risk of speculating that instinctual economy has death as its point of departure. Instinct would then tend towards an initial state where there is a total absence of tension. This hypothesis attributes vital phenomena to reactions of the organism to external accidents constituting obstacles on the path towards its death.[9] In short, the tension evoked in inanimate things by the action of a force, as unfathomable as the force responsible for the big bang, is seeking an outlet. This tendency defines the first instinct, that of return to the inanimate, which was the initial state. But external influences interfere with this and "[…] oblige the still surviving substance to diverge ever more widely from its original course of life and to make ever more complicated detours before reaching its aim of death. These circuitous paths to death, faithfully kept to by the conservative instincts, would thus ultimately form the picture of the phenomena of life" (Freud, 1920g, p. 39).

The living substance registers the detours caused by external influences, and integrates them in its internal system to such an extent that they become instincts of self-preservation whose function is to assure that the organism will follow its own path to death. When Freud writes that "[T]hese guardians of life, too, were originally the myrmidons[10] of death," he portrays an organism determined to draw its energy from forces opposed to it. In other words, based on this daring hypothesis, the living organism is driven by a death instinct striving towards an earlier state, but draws its energy from that unfathomable force which originally disturbed inanimate matter. On the path towards its aim, the death instinct meets with obstacles that it has learned to incorporate before continuing on its course. In this light, the phenomena of life appear as a multitude of detours on the path towards death. These circumvolutions, then, are the form taken by the life of an organism conditioned to ward off the danger of arriving at death otherwise than in its own fashion.

Hence arises the paradoxical situation that the living organism struggles most energetically against events (dangers in fact) which might help it to attain its life's aim (death) rapidly—by a kind of short circuit.

This paradox opens a door that Freud quickly closes. This door provided a glimpse of a paradoxical system made up of a primary cohesive force and an inconceivable force which disturbs it. The original inertia was seeking an earlier state, but on the path back to it certain external events impeded its progress; these events were transformed into compulsory detours. And these detours became forces of self-preservation. In this configuration, "life" appears as the end result of forces of attraction and restraint which form a veritable paradoxical system. Having come so far, Freud could have based the concept of psychosomatic life on a model no longer dependent on the paradigm of presence, or the idea of the natural. But in the next sentence he draws back, changes direction, and returns to the common sense of instinctual duality and to the paradigm of presence. "But let us pause for a moment and reflect. It cannot be so."[11] What he is saying to his readers, in fact, is: let's be reasonable, death cannot constitute an instinctual economy, we cannot seriously say that the point of departure of psychosexual life is death.

Having ventured onto territory where men of science could not follow, Freud repeatedly asked the reader to forgive him for having taken them on such a journey,[12] and asked, in fact, to be forgiven for having gone so far as to imagine a *death* instinct. It is true that an institution, that of psychoanalytic discourse, can hardly lean on the tip of a paradox for support. The larger foundation provided by dualism is necessary if teachers are to instruct students interested in psychoanalytic "knowledge". As soon as he undertakes to tame his own daring, Freud reinvents an improvised instinctual duality by separating the sexual instincts from all the others.[13]

When Freud, the adventurous researcher, is brought back to reason by the other Freud, a follower of Auguste Comte, the paradoxical system which is a single instinct, the result of a life-and-death instinct and of external events, is transformed into a conflict between life instincts and death instincts. But, while Freud subdues his theory, he does not take back the clinical breakthrough he brought about in the meantime. The rift that this has created between theory and practice has never been mended. Clinical practice—let us say, rather, the theory of practice—disposes of a fundamental concept, a *Grundbegriff*, consisting of "repetition compulsion", the outcome of a paradoxical reasoning that could be expressed as follows: the life instinct is a drive towards death which is transformed and delayed by external events. This concept is in sharp contrast with the dualism that was to remain the foundation of psychoanalytic theory for a century. Since 1919, clinical practice has been dominated by the discovery of the compulsion of the *psyche-soma* to tie every external event into the psyche, regardless of whether an event helps or hinders its progression. But this key concept of practice has remained bereft of its theoretical equivalent. It is as if clinical practice can rely, without admitting it, on a paradoxical model, while theory, which normally should reflect practice, remains tied to a model which excludes the paradoxical.

What is left of the death instinct is a residue of this discarded reflection, an idea which, outside the context where it appeared, has neither theoretical nor clinical interest. Despite Freud's attempt to put it to a different use, this idea has lost its sense. When Freud abandoned the life-and-death instinct, he let go of the tip of a splendid theoretical glacier that his concern with common sense erased from the map as soon as it was discovered. The abandoned moraine became an aggressive, destructive impulse. As a result, it became possible to accept stupid explanations of accidents, of war, of delinquency, of drug addiction, and of suicide: they were simply ascribed to the "death instinct". This explanation, however, is merely a sign of unfinished thinking.

When we speak of bringing primary conditions to transference, we transpose to the field of analytic treatment the idea that establishing the periodicity between the current of innervation and the current of erasure, which is vital for the psychic apparatus, depends on the primary relation between mother and child. What Freud refers to as secondary process coincides with primary process. Restraint, scansion, and inhibition are as primary as seduction, incitement, and facilitation. A normal mother offers the child a rhythm made up of a sequence of signs, separated by clear caesuras. In all the sensory fields, periods of incitement *and* restraint progress smoothly, and the grid formed by this criss-crossing of little rivers of signs that stop and flow in similar *tempi* sketches the outline of the ego. To illustrate this, we could imagine a psychic entity belonging to both mother and child, and presiding over the economy of their paradoxical unity. This entity is a transitional psychic matrix.

Notes

1. The author is indebted to Loup Verlet for pointing out the importance of the paradoxical model. In *La malle de Newton* (1993), Loup Verlet describes the founding paradox that Newton buried in the *Principia*, which seems to emerge from actual experience.

2. We gave our attention to the fiction of a primitive psychical apparatus whose activity was regulated by the attempt to avoid the build-up of excitation [...]—felt as unpleasure [...]. The first wishing was perhaps a hallucinatory charging of the memory of satisfaction. However, this hallucination, if it was not to be retained to the point of exhaustion, turned out to be no good at bringing about the cessation of the need [...].

   This made a second activity—in our terms, the activity of a second system—necessary, which does not allow the memory-charge to get as far as perception and from there to bind the forces of the psyche, but diverts the excitation caused by the need along a detour; this indirect route ultimately alters the external world in such a way that a real perception of the object of satisfaction can come about [...]. [...] the two systems are the germ of [...] the unconscious and the preconscious. (Freud, 1900a, p. 598).

3. By "primary process" Freud means a mode of functioning of the psychic apparatus in which psychic energy flows freely from one representation to another, guided by the mechanisms of condensation and displacement, without regard for sense, with the sole aim of satisfaction, and taking the shortest route.

4. The theory of psychoneuroses asserts as an indisputable and invariable fact that only sexual wishful impulses from infancy, which have undergone repression [...] are thus able to furnish the motive force for the formation of psychoneurotic symptoms. [...] Dreams themselves are among the manifestations of this suppressed material; [...]. (Freud, 1900a, pp. 605–608).

5. This led to a notion of the archaic character of dreams that was to pervade psychoanalytic doctrine for many years, preparing the way for the resurgence of ontology in the theory, and therefore in the way analysts regarded their patients. The latter's symptoms were attributed to archaic impulses.

6. This passage is inspired by Jacques Derrida in *Writing and Difference* (1978).

7. This agrees with a notion which I have long had about the method in which the perceptual apparatus of our mind functions, but which I have hitherto kept to myself. My theory was that cathectic innervation [*Besetzunginnervation*] is sent out and withdrawn in rapid periodic impulses from within into the completely pervious system *Pcpt.-Cs.* [*zurückgezogen*]. So long as that system is cathected in this manner, it receives perceptions (which are accompanied by consciousness) and passes the excitation on to the unconscious mnemic systems; but as soon as the cathexis is withdrawn, consciousness is extinguished and

the functioning of the system comes to a standstill. It is as though the unconscious stretches out feelers, through the medium of the system Pcpt.-Cs., towards the external world and hastily withdraws them as soon as they have sampled the excitations coming from it. Thus the interruptions, which in the case of the Mystic Pad have an external origin, were attributed by my hypothesis to the discontinuity in the current of innervations; and the actual breaking of contact which occurs in the Mystic Pad was replaced in my theory by the periodic non-excitability of the perceptual system. I further had a suspicion that this discontinuous method of functioning of the system Pcpt.-Cs. lies at the bottom of the origin of the concept of time. (Freud, 1925a, pp. 227–234).

8. Traces thus produce the space of their inscription only by acceding to the period of their erasure. From the beginning, […] they are constituted by the double force of repetition and erasure, legibility and illegibility. (Derrida, 1978, p. 226).

9. The elementary living entity would from its very beginning have had no wish to change. […] Let us suppose, then, that all the organic instincts are conservative […] and tend towards the restoration of an earlier state of things […]. Every modification which is thus imposed upon the course of the organism's life is […] stored up for further repetition. Those instincts are therefore bound to give a deceptive appearance of being forces tending towards change […], whilst in fact they are merely seeking to reach an ancient goal … (Freud, 1920g, p. 39).

10. Myrmidons are foot soldiers providing assistance to the knight.

11. "*Aber besinnen wir uns, es kann nicht so sein.*" in the original.

12. The reader should not overlook the fact that what follows is the development of an extreme line of thought. Later on, when account is taken of the sexual instincts, it will be found that the necessary limitations and corrections are applied to it. (Freud, 1920g, p. 39, footnote added 1925).

13. These germ-cells, therefore, work against the death of the living substance and succeed in winning for it what we can only regard as potential immortality […]. We must regard as in the highest degree significant the fact that this function of the germ-cell is reinforced, or only made possible, if it coalesces with another cell similar to itself and yet differing from it. (Freud, 1920g, p. 39).

CHAPTER FIVE

A transitional psychic matrix

Breath, you poem beyond all seeing!
Pure and ceaseless demi-urge
in counterpoise with our own being.
Interchange in which I rhythmically emerge.

—Rilke, *Sonnets to Orpheus* (1922)

When Circe warned him of the danger of the call of the Sirens for his sailors, Ulysses had their ears filled with wax and had himself tightly bound to the mast of his ship. Still following Circe's advice, Ulysses enjoined his mate to tighten his bonds when, under the spell of the monstrous creatures, he would beg to be untied. In this situation, Ulysses is at once seduced by the song of the Sirens, and kept tied to the mast by his mate. Circe who restrains and the Sirens who attract illustrate a paradoxical system in which the hero is both seduced and restrained. The important element of this system is the copula that separates and unites attraction and restraint. In this light, Ulysses is not subjected to seduction and restraint, but is, rather, an element of a paradoxical system that carries him beyond the point of absolute danger. In this position, he is torn but he escapes and is carried beyond (literally, in Greek, *metapherein*) the place where death awaits him.

According to my reading, this segment of Homer's poetic saga becomes the illustration of the fundamental rhythmic sequence serving to form the earliest sketch of the subject and of instinct.[1] This preliminary sketch is composed of a series of sensory incitement signs, subsequently organised into a sequence by means of scansion. In this sequence, signs equivalent to the song of the Sirens combine with signs equivalent to the bonds tying Ulysses to the mast. Such a sequence is a basic paradoxical unit. It has no meaning by itself, but it creates the virtual space where continuity and discontinuity unite, and where instinct originates. This tying together is the condition necessary for sense,[2] and the subject involved in this condition will not remember it. Here we are dealing with the origin, with what Hegel called "the negation of the negation". Being tied to the mast—first negation—abolishes the call to abolition contained in the song of the Sirens—second negation. What is "not posited", the original being, is erased and preserved—the dialectical *Aufhebung*—in this space which is the point of origin of instinct. Thus, the primary instinct abolishes and preserves the origin (Jarszyk, 1999; Sloterdijk, 1997).

Finding the source of this other sense is a quest dating back to the time when man started to search for his beginnings in the mirror of reflection. All major mythological systems attempting to account for man's origins attest to this search and constitute its archives. As we have seen, Freud locates in the unconscious a paradoxical continuity-discontinuity system likely to give rise to periodicity.[3] By positing this theory, Freud makes the paradoxical system a universal given; the question concerning what conditions are favourable or unfavourable to the creation of such a system is submerged in the concept of the unconscious. Like all founders, and particularly like Newton, Freud places his theoretical ground far from the origin.

My hypothesis is that this periodic nature, this ability to function in a paradoxical continuous-discontinuous mode, is indeed characteristic of living species, but that the human species, unlike other animals, does not have the benefit of instant agreement between this natural condition and its expressions. Human beings are gifted with speech and have the ability to think; but with this faculty comes exclusion from the realm of the inherent. Man's particularity in relation to all other animal species consists in the fact that agreement between what is natural to him and his thinking process is never established once and for all, and always remains to be created.[4] Human beings are distinct in that they are able to say something different than that which is expressed variously by the body. Man can lie to his body. The nocturnal butterfly whose hearing is exclusively attuned to sounds emitted by its predator, the bat, retreats when the enemy approaches (Uexküll, 2010). Man, on the other hand, can interpret signs of danger, can register them but misunderstand, or insist on misinterpreting them. While animals receive a somatic-emotional matrix, man receives a somatic-psychic matrix. And the accuracy with which this matrix responds to external solicitation depends on the primary conditions with which the child is provided, that is, on the mother's ability to express harmoniously and in unison the different languages in which she addresses the child, speech included.

The early sketch of the subject seems to emerge naturally when maternal languages, that of the voice and that of the arm, for example, or that of the voice and that of facial expression have the same rhythm.[5] This early sketch is consolidated by the similarity of the rhythm of the flow of the voice and the flow of milk. The rhythm of the voice draws an outline, that of the breast draws an outline, that of the arm draws an outline, and they are similar.[6] But when the voice draws a different outline than the breast, nourishment ceases. The early sketch of the child's ego emerges as he is being nourished by the vocal outline which surrounds him. The homogeneous quality of the flow of the mother's different language sequences draws this early sketch. The voice, the breast, and the arm can send different messages, but they express them in the same rhythmic form. These rhythmic sequences have a binary structure in which "one" stands for incitement and "zero" stands for scansion. This abstract image serves to illustrate that an acoustic sequence can create an outline, just like a visual, tactile, or vestibular incitement can. This rhythmic unison of the mother's different languages instils in the child a feeling of permanence, confidence, and security. These experiences create the ability to pass from one language to another, from one state to another.

The feeling of permanence of the self-image, the locus of the subject, an absolute requirement for suffering, for dreaming, and for fantasy, finds the condition necessary for its existence in the coming together of two languages. A fragment from Sophocles' *Philoctetes* illustrates this necessity: the hero is abandoned on his island by the Atrides, his companions, because his wound exudes a foul odour. But the Atrides need his marvellous bow to conquer the Trojans. Neoptolemus, who is sent as an envoy, negotiates with Philoctetes and convinces him to give up his marvellous bow, his most precious possession and his only means of survival on the island. When Philoctetes feels the pain caused by his wound returning, he begs his new friend not to leave him alone.

PHILOCTETES: *... This visitor comes sharply but goes quickly. Only, I beseech you, do not leave me alone.*
NEOPTOLEMUS: *Fear not, we will remain.*
PHILOCTETES: *You will remain?*
NEOPTOLEMUS: *Be sure of it.*
PHILOCTETES: *Well, I do not ask to put you on your oath, my son.*
NEOPTOLEMUS: *Rest satisfied. It is not lawful for me to go without you.*
PHILOCTETES: *Your hand for pledge!*
                    ("Embale kheiros pistin")
NEOPTOLEMUS: *I give it, to stay.*

[Philoctetes cries out in pain and crumbles to the ground ...]

NEOPTOLEMUS: *Come friends, let us leave him in quietness, that he may fall on slumber.* (p. 253)

The word given by the friend is guaranteed in another form of language: in this case, the giving of the hand. For the hero to find rest, he needs the assurance given by a message transmitted in two languages. In the case of the mother, the "giving of the hand" is equivalent to the correspondence between a word and a gesture, a word and a tone of voice, the content and the form, the spoken message and the feel of the arm.

Literature provides us with another example of the importance of the coherence of languages: when Proust (1918) describes the concordance of the languages produced on stage by the great actress "La Berma" in the role of Phaedra, comparing this harmony with the discordant body language of the actress playing Aricia, he gives a perfect illustration of the difference, for a child, between feeling that he is held by a caregiver whose languages are in tune with each other, and feeling held by an out-of-tune mother.[7]

How does the mother bring coherence to all the languages she uses to address the child? To develop this idea, let us use the hypothesis of a transitional psychic matrix which governs the recognition of the child. The mother recognises in the real child the child she perceived in this psychic, dream-like image. This matrix guides her in her adjustment to the child, and also serves as a mediating device through which the child recognises the emotions and sensations he experiences. In fact, it would be more accurate to say "he was to experience", since these sensations only exist—only become located physically and temporally—because they prefigured in a psychic matrix.

The child cries and the mother feels pain to which she attributes a cause using the dream-like child as a model. Once heard, the cry is given interpretation by the transitional entity, and is instantly inscribed in a semiotic space where it becomes the sign of a need: the need to eat, for example. When pain and need are embodied, an event is transformed into a sign through the reflection projected by this transitional entity. The events re-embodied[8] through the mother's adaptation to the image she perceives in this shared *psyche* (mirror). Pierre Delaunay (1989) uses the term "a psychic device for two", a fitting term in the context which concerns us. Although it is the mother who draws the initial outline of the psychic matrix, very soon, even before the birth of the child, mother and child start to build this matrix together.

Wittgenstein (1978) asks what could be the meaning of "I have a toothache" and, above all, the meaning of "I understand you when you say: 'I have a toothache'". "I have a toothache" can only be conceived, can only be expressed because the dream-like child of the transitional matrix anticipated the toothache. The toothache was already there before the real child felt it; it existed as a virtual element of the matrix, an element waiting to be embodied, to be re-presented, although the matrix presented it already. The toothache script was already written before the ego presented it on stage. What we are saying about toothache also applies to hunger, cold, thirst, and all the sensations that have no existence in themselves, *per se*, but that are presented and felt in advance by the child of the psychic matrix before being felt and re-presented by the ego of the child. This allows us to say that the transitional image is the condition of the *Einfuhlung*, of this "sympathy" Wittgenstein finds so problematic.

By translating the cries of the child into the language of the transitional matrix, the mother feels the pain of the child. Because she is able to create the suffering of the child by recognising it in the mirror of the psychic matrix, the mother brings this suffering into existence and gives it to the child. By bearing it, she calms the child, while letting him help to calm her. Thus, she is the object, and no longer solely the subject, in the process of calming the child. A harmonious musical score is played in unison by mother and child, by the transitional matrix and the mother.

To illustrate the role of the child in this musical ensemble, we go back to the first incident of disagreement between maternal response and the rhythm of the child. The first time the mother notices this disjunction, takes it upon herself, and recognises her inability to prevent all breaks in rhythm, the child is given the primary experience of being able to move his mother, to affect her, to enter her internality.[9] This initial dissonance registered by the mother is fundamental, because it is at once a sign of the fallibility of maternal attention, and of her ability to recognise this flaw *and* be ready to correct it.

When the mother accepts her inability to prevent all the breaks in rhythm, when she bears them, she creates the conditions necessary both for the inscription of the child in a semiotic space, and for the creation of a boundary between him and her. This acceptance provides support for the separation from without and from within, and is the foundation of the first distinction between good and bad. By accepting dissonance, the mother bestows the gift of the negative, of discontinuity, of the trace of death, of the bad, which she takes upon herself. As a result, the child can distinguish between the external which is bad and the internal which is good. The original separation between outside and inside finds its place, and the foundations of self-esteem are laid in this act of recognition by the mother of the first disjunction, and thanks to her ability to give the child the vital illusion that he has repaired it himself.

Once the alternation between broken continuity and re-established continuity has been achieved, the child can bear disharmony not only between his mother's rhythm and his own, but between the different languages of the mother. He can now perceive and signal dissonance between the language of the arm, of the hand, of the voice, and of the speech. At this point, it becomes possible to speak of a relation between the mother and the child.

The transitional psychic matrix is both internal and external to the ego.[10] The fact that the mother carries within her a dream-double of the child allows her to recognise the real child and separate from him. The fact that the child has two locations is what allows him access to a human world. The "matrix child" allows the mother to see the child she felt in her womb. Without him, she would not be able to recognise the child who is born. Without the mirror of her dream, the child would seem monstrous to her.[11] Everything the "matrix child" did not experience, feel, think, each thing for which he was not the scene, such as jealousy, hate, mourning, or any other mundane object, will appear monstrous to the mother and, consequently, to the child. Such objects will be traumatic and will provoke anxiety or panic, splitting or disintegration, depending on the degree of absence from the transitional matrix.[12] The mother only perceives what her dream has anticipated. The dream-like child guides her towards the real child in whom she recognises her dream.

Every crucial moment of human existence calls upon the transitional matrix that governs the passage from foetal life to breathing life, from childhood to adolescence, from adolescence to adulthood. At these critical times, the flexibility, the anticipatory capacity, and the richness of the transitional matrix are solicited for support. Every trial and every leap in human life is an occasion when this matrix could fail. A rigid matrix, cluttered with imposed images, will not facilitate passages and their resolution. These occasions create conditions which can produce symptoms as serious as a psychotic break, since the child's interlocutor is none other than the "matrix child".

The flexibility of the matrix and the mother's ability to adapt to the child are flawed when an event in the mother's life, or in the life of someone preceding her in the family line, has created a gap in the psychic matrix. In that case, the child is face to face with an imposed figure that blocks access to this gap. This guardian expresses himself in one of the maternal languages: for instance, her arm follows a rhythm different than the rhythm of her voice. A stranger has stepped in between mother and child. When the mother is completely determined to disregard the disagreement between the languages in which she speaks to the child, this dissonance affects the child.

I once shared a train compartment with a young mother and her baby. Our travel conditions were not ideal. Suddenly, the baby cried out, but the mother had no way to warm up his bottle. Instead, she took a sip of cold milk from the bottle and, after warming it in her mouth, she transferred it directly into the baby's mouth. The baby closed his eyes and registered an expression the mother interpreted as a smile. She smiled back and, this time, the baby's answering expression was a closer imitation of her smile.

Let us suppose that the same mother becomes distracted, and her attention wanders. The child is annoyed and cries. The mother understands instantly what happened. She rocks the child while warming another mouthful of milk. She gives him the warm milk and sings him a song that tells the story of a naughty mother who was letting her thoughts dwell on this and that, instead of thinking about her baby. When she finishes the song, the child falls asleep.

Now let us imagine a mother who simply swallows the mouthful of milk. She is thinking about something else. And the thought she swallowed is so painful that she does not understand why the baby continues to cry. She does not understand her baby's cry. She has swallowed the thought, the pain in the thought, the mouthful of milk, and even the memory of the mixture of thought and milk. So the baby who continues to cry bothers her. "Is he sick?" I'll have to take him to a doctor, he must be coming down with something …" Or, "It will do him good to cry a little … he'll learn."

This child has no choice but to become the subject of rhythmic dissonance. When the parent does not recognise the part he plays in the scene he does not know he is enacting with the child, when he withdraws, he eliminates the witness he could have been for the child. At that very instant, the child becomes the author of rhythmic dissonance, and places himself at the source of an excitation that must come from somewhere. A stimulus must have a source, and when the parent does not recognise dissonance, the latter becomes a constant excitation. This characteristic of instinct, as defined by Freud, allows us to say that an instinctual source was created in the child. When the parent refuses to witness[13] the sensation he has brought about, the child substitutes himself for the parent. As a result of this disavowal that refuses to witness his sensation, the child loses his place as the object of someone's affection and, at the same time, loses his position as a subject of concerted action.

When the other avoids involvement, the child splits off, not only as Ferenczi (2002) thought, into a sleeping child and a child who watches over him, but also into a demon who perpetuates the source of constant excitation produced by the inscription in his body of the censured event. The child involuntarily enacts the discord which has gone unnoticed, and he repeats it using the means of expression at his disposal at a particular age. If he is a few months old, he will present—as one would present a defence—acute dehydration. Later, he might present a phobic symptom, refusal to do schoolwork or attend school, or he will develop anorexia nervosa.

Incorporation of the witness who avoids involvement takes place at the level of sexual enjoyment. When a parent refuses to witness the child's sensations, the child can have recourse to a desperate recovery of his active and passive paradoxical assets, components of the "id-ego". Sexual enjoyment re-establishes his position as subject of an act of reparation, as well as his passive position as object of someone's affection.

The fantasies Freud ascribed to an "Oedipus" present in each child appear when the psychic matrix has been transformed into a screen and when the image projected on this screen is one the child cannot deal with. Sometimes, in some circumstances, an "imposed figure" appears and discourages the child from participating in a unifying movement. The child cannot play with such a figure so as to create a new reality; the only thing he can do is swallow it. Instead of receiving an invitation to create something virtual among an infinity of possibilities, the child only "receives" the totem erected in the maternal dream. As a result, the child is both wounded and attracted into an incestuous relationship.

The parent and the child remain connected by this invisible Siamese abnormality. The fact that the matrix produces no reflection creates a continuous entity. In this place, the distance given the thing by the name is missing. When an event is not reflected in the psychic matrix, the inside-outside duality is erased at that location.[14] This situation has countless variations, all of which are hidden clinical forms of incest. These forms might be considered minor if their effects were not at times more incapacitating than the incestuous crimes brought before the courts.

Notes

1. The disappearance and return of this moment constitute the condition of memory. This is the "birth trauma" that Otto Rank intuited but did not elaborate.
2. This sequence resembles the rite described by Marcel Mauss as a set of signs with a beginning, a middle, and an end. Those who continued Mauss's work have shown that in some religions the ritual has greater value than the myth. In the Vedic religion, for instance, myths are variable and loosely defined, while the syntactic organisation of rituals is clearly established. As is the case for rituals, the paradoxical system

formed by such sequences does not produce sense, but is a required condition for sense. On this aspect of ritual, see Staal, 1983.

3. This idea is presented as incidental in the above quoted "A Note upon the 'Mystic Writing-Pad'". In his "A Project for a Scientific Psychology" (1950a), Freud had already presented this contradiction, saying that "[A] discontinuous or periodic temporality ... is the only way out of the difficulty." But what is the origin of this "period"? In 1895, Freud saw it as proceeding from the excitation period transmitted to the perception neurones. Thirty years later, in the "Note" (1925a), it was as if this period originated in the unconscious.

4. See the work of Pierre Legendre.

5. Here, "rhythm" is intended to be taken in the sense the Presocratics gave the term, as Emile Benveniste points out in *Problems in General Linguistics* (1973). In our context, "rhythm" refers to the shape taken by a living entity in its mobility, not to the metric character of Socratic philosophy which identifies and describes ideas, that is, still forms.

6. The sense of unity, the feeling of having one's "own space" is produced by this rhythmic harmony.

7. Berma's arms, which the lines of verse themselves, by the same emissive force that made the voice issue from her lips, seemed to raise on to her bosom like leaves displaced by a gush of water; her stage presence [...] she had gradually built up [...] based upon reasonings that hat lost their original deliberation, had melted into a sort of radiance whereby they sent throbbing, round the person of the heroine, rich and complex elements which the fascinated spectator nevertheless took not for a triumph of dramatic artistry but for a manifestation of life; those white veils themselves, which, tenuous and clinging, seemed to be of a living substance and to have been woven by the suffering [...] around which they drew themselves like a frail and shrinking cocoon—all these, voice, posture, gestures, veils round this embodiment of an idea which a line of poetry is, [...] were merely additional envelopes which, instead of concealing, showed up in greater splendour the soul that had assimilated them to itself and had spread itself through them [...]. (Proust, 1918, pp. 44–45).

Berma's fellow-actors, on the other hand, are far from achieving such perfection and are judged without pity:

> Similarly the gestures of the players said to their arms, to their garments: "Be majestic." But the unsubmissive limbs allowed a biceps which knew nothing of the part to flaunt itself between shoulder and elbow; they continued to express the triviality of everyday life and to bring into prominence, instead of fine shades

of Racinian meaning, mere muscular relationships; and the draperies which they held up fell back again along vertical lines in which the natural law that governs falling bodies was challenged only by an insipid textile pliancy. (Proust, 1918, p. 42)

8. This expression is borrowed from Merleau-Ponty (1964).
9. Jacques Lévine sees this as the crucial moment when the child experiences penetrating the mother.
10. In Platonic discourse, this idea is equivalent to place, *khôra*. *Khôra*, place, enclosed space, is an entity defining a basic characteristic of the being, just like "same" and "other". "Place" is something of a different order than "same" and "other", but it is the condition of their existence. *Khôra* is the condition of distancing, of the separation between "same" and "other". This entity is the subject of a study by Jacques Derrida in *On the Name* (1992a).
11. R. Polanski's movie *Rosemary's Baby* portrays such a catastrophe.
12. I felt that the patient had experienced in infancy a mother who dutifully responded to the infant's emotional displays [...]. [But] from the infant's point of view she should have taken into her, and thus experienced, the fear that the child was dying. (Bion, 1967).
13. Here, the root of "detest" is to be taken from the Latin *testor*, "I bear witness", the sense François Villon gives it in his poem *Le Grand Testament* (1461), which is his testimony.
14. This absence of reflection produces a gap in the protective shield, a notion which will be defined in the next chapter.

CHAPTER SIX

An origin between absorption and expulsion

He who seeks does not find, but he who does not seek will be found.

—Franz Kafka, "*The Third Notebook*" (1917)

Once Freud had adopted the idea that sexual fantasies triggered by endogenous drives were traumatic in themselves, the question of why they were more traumatic for some individuals than for others was swept away by the tidal wave of natural philosophy. From then on, the ability to repress the Oedipus complex was considered to depend in part on the strength of endogenous drives, seen as variable from one person to another. This concession to the theory of individual constitution was to leave future generations of psychoanalysts with the task of reducing the role of a notion inherited from the nineteenth century. They would have to try to humanise these individual differences by identifying, with Winnicott, that which concerns the maternal context and, with Ferenczi, Nicolas Abraham, and Jacques Lacan, the non-elaborated pain of previous generations.

The idea of psychic trauma was the first means used to contest Freud's newly formulated fantasy theory. War traumas provided Ferenczi with the clinical opportunity to review the initial version of the doctrine. Freud himself participated in this review. In 1920, *Beyond the Pleasure Principle* allowed clinical theory to take a big step forward thanks to the discovery that living beings tend to repeat a situation that has not yet had a satisfactory resolution. But at the very moment when he provided clinical practice with a decisive opening, Freud forfeited the theoretical contribution associated with it: for the sake of common sense, he abandoned the idea of a single death-and-life instinct, and returned to the instinctual duality composed of a life instinct and a death instinct, or of sexual instincts and ego instincts.

This decision to ignore his own theoretical contribution set the stage for Freud's break with Ferenczi, which was to occur ten years later. The same decision resulted in the setting aside of the writings where Ferenczi was developing a theory of clinical practice still very valuable today. But the questions left unanswered when Freud abandoned his initial idea continued to occasion intense research activity throughout the subsequent evolution of the psychoanalytic movement. Eventually, two opposing camps came into existence: on the one hand, psychoanalysts who looked for the origin of their patients' suffering in unconscious sexual fantasies; and on the other, those who searched for this origin in the consequences of traumatic events. This opposition sparked valuable research, but it also engendered fruitless controversy between those who claimed to find in the "unconscious" of a sexual trauma victim the traces of a repressed desire to be subjected to such an event, and those who rejected this judgment and threw out fantasy theory with this ill-intentioned interpretation.[1]

Yet, in *Beyond the Pleasure Principle*, Freud gives a precise definition of trauma, in which he makes a clear distinction between container and content, conditions of sense and sense itself. When he describes as traumatic "any excitations from outside which are powerful enough to break through the protective shield"—the only definition of the traumatic found in his work—Freud distinguishes a container and a content separated by an invisible skin he calls the protective shield. This conception is compatible with his theory of the psyche, where sexual instincts assail the ego from the inside, but he now links this new definition of the traumatic with a different concept of the sexual than the one he used previously. In fact, when he asserts that a "mechanical" external stimulus should be considered a source of sexual excitation, when he supposes that intense, painful sensations not connected psychically, "not directly felt", find sexual resolution, Freud transforms the sexual into the language into which any break-in can be translated.

This revelation has extensive ramifications. As soon as the conceptual framework of psychoanalysis was no longer seen as founded on a certain "something" inherent and already present, as soon as the sexual was seen as the accomplishment of human process, the result of a specifically human activity capable of sublimating all differential tension, when the sexual finally appeared as one of the privileged modes man has of dealing with that which breaks through the protective shield, theoretical ground shifted from what philosophers call "being" to what can be called "difference". In this new light, the sexual assumes the task of humanising all accidents and of correcting all failures of symbolisation. Any pain which has not attained the more elaborate status of psychic suffering can find an outlet in the sexual. The sexual symbolises that which cannot be symbolised. In addition, when the sexual is no longer considered a primitive, congenital factor, but rather a primary reaction to a trauma, fantasy can be reconciled with trauma theory. And the two theories, "trauma theory" and "fantasy theory", are no longer in conflict. Fantasy can be understood as the story the subject tells himself in order to consolidate an enjoyment inscribed as a trace in his body, but not consciously remembered. Fantasy is post-traumatic testimony to sexual enjoyment.

But, like Moses who was never to see the Land of Milk and Honey himself, Freud was not to discover the field of psychoanalytic practice based on *difference*. He was to remain fascinated by his first discoveries, and unable to forego the certainties conferred by the paradigm of presence. And yet, he did not erase his own daring hypotheses. He was content to laugh at himself and say that they were contrary to common sense. Thus, the paths opened by the notion of a death (-and-life) instinct, and by the sexual seen as a privileged method of humanising traumatic excitations, were to remain unexplored. Because he abandoned this research, Freud did not continue to develop the notion of trauma as it would have been shaped by the new definition of the sexual. He put an end to this line of thought even before reflecting on the nature and origin of the protective shield.

In fact, while Freud describes this protective shield and defines its function, he says nothing about its nature or its point of origin. He thinks of it as a thick covering, like skin hardened by calluses and bereft of memory. When this protective shield, whose intense latent energy cannot be mobilised, is infiltrated by organic pain—this is the example Freud uses—free libidinal energy becomes concentrated in the area where the pain has penetrated. This free energy, obtained at the expense of the other psychic systems, serves to offset the pain and to repair the local damage done to the protective shield. Although these images are suggestive, neither Freud nor his successors made any assertions concerning the origin of this protective covering.

What I am proposing is that an original, consistent paradoxical system can explain the nature of the protective shield. The paradoxical system develops in conditions where absorption and expulsion forces coexist. In these conditions, the child is exposed to forces which both attract and restrain him. Since every child is at once Little Red Riding-Hood and Hop o' My Thumb, he is also afraid of being eaten by the wolf: absorbed, and of being abandoned in the forest; expelled. We use these fairy tales as imaginary representations of these two forces of absorption and expulsion in which the child resides in a potentially variable but always positive sphere. A normal child is subjected to a multitude of seduction and restraint stimuli, in short, to a paradoxical system whose nucleus, the basic paradoxical unit, is composed of a series of incitements punctuated by a scansion which organises them retroactively into a sequence. Discontinuity paradoxically carries within it the promise of repetition: it is the principle of cohesion and consistency. The sequences follow each other with continuity *and* discontinuity, like a breath of the *psyche-soma*.

We consider this sphere where continuity and discontinuity combine to be every child's natural endowment. In order for it to come to fruition, the child has to meet a parent who lets him "come upon himself" (Rilke, 1898). When such a parent absorbs and expels, seduces and restrains, he is in tune with the paradoxical endowment with which the child is potentially gifted. The resonance between this primary maternal disposition, which is far from natural, and the child's natural potential is what creates the illusion that the newborn's need is self-evident.

What capital does the mother draw on to expel the child and to associate discontinuity with the vital movement of continuity? She draws on the capital of her own death. By bringing a child into the world, a parent erases his own death and expels it into the child. Through his objection to death, his own, the parent involves the child in this death which he erases. From that moment on, the child carries the trace—albeit erased—of the thrown off thing. He carries the trace of radical otherness, of death, something specifically human, existing for mankind alone. The expulsion of the child is equivalent to a primary "no". In this "no", in the mother's cry at birth, there is a shadow of death, of a death thrown off into the child and for him. This expulsion is accompanied by an opposite movement of absorption through which the parent attempts to annul discontinuity and reconstruct lost continuity. The shadow of death also appears in the movement of absorption, but in another guise: that of praise, of song, of seduction. The trace of death is doubly present: in the yearning for undifferentiation, for the reconstitution of the unit, as well as in its opposite, the movement towards distinction and separation. These two tendencies, with their corresponding mythical figures, account for the origin.

In the *Odyssey*, the one who seduces the hero, who sings his praises and invites him to become one with her, is the Siren. The one who restrains him by advising that he have himself tied to the mast while the Siren woos him with her song is Circe. Her advice is what gives Ulysses the strength and support he needs to continue his journey to the end. By contrast, his sailors, who do not hear the song of the Sirens because their ears are filled with wax, all perish prematurely.

In the following passage from Genesis, the two figures blend into the figure of God, who pronounces the injunction to eat and not to eat, and who holds out death at the same time:

> And the Lord God commanded the man, saying: Of every tree of the garden thou mayest freely eat, but of the tree of the knowledge of good and evil, thou shalt not eat of it, for in the day that thou eatest thereof thou shalt surely die. (Genesis II: 16–17)

This double injunction implies that humanity must at once eat of the tree of knowledge—included in "every tree of the garden"—and not eat of it. God does not command man to eat of every tree of the garden *except* the tree of knowledge, but rather to eat of every tree of the garden *and* not to eat of the tree of knowledge.[2] This is not an injunction accompanied by a death threat, but rather a paradoxical injunction which immediately places man in the situation of eating *and* not eating. The fact that the word "die" appears for the first time in this passage does not mean that until then animals did not die, or that their death was not real. What it means is that the equivalent for life in animals is the indivisible "death-and-life" given to humans. Man alone has a representation of his finitude because, being the only living creature endowed with speech, he can bring into existence that which disappears from his sight. Things present themselves to animals; man alone can re-present them to himself. Man is to be aware of his mortality, bury his dead, and remember them. He shall be the only living creature to inhabit the paradoxical sphere of living-and-dying. In the next chapter of Genesis, the figure of the seducer is reinforced by that of the serpent whose appearance both eliminates and brings out (*Aufhebung*) the paradox of the divine word. In metapsychological terms, we could say that the instinct and aptitude for guilt eliminates and brings out the original paradox.

In the story of Abraham, the paradoxical injunction is renewed and brought to a climax. Abraham is enjoined to put *and* not to put his son to death. His trial is that of the parent asked to re-enact the scene of the origin, where he threw off his own death onto the child, and to take it back upon himself. This passage, called Abraham's Sacrifice, Isaac's Sacrifice, or The Tying Up of Isaac, is an account of the ultimate test man has to face before his death. Abraham is asked to take back death, which he had thrown off by expelling the child in order to seduce him into living. Enjoined to sacrifice his son and not to sacrifice him, he vanquishes his own death once more, the death that is his alone[3] and that he had thrown off onto his son by expelling him, happy in the knowledge of the continuity ensured by this birth. The rest of the text confirms this reading, since it is a ram that presents itself for sacrifice, instead of the lamb Abraham was expecting. Abraham immediately offers God this sacrificial animal, adult like him, "in the place of his son". Through this rite, he offers God the sacrifice of the immortality he thought he achieved with Isaac's birth. Abraham celebrates the death of the adult and takes it upon himself; he agrees to respect the order of generations and this submission is the sign that he has passed the paradoxical test imposed by divine law.

If we want to conjugate these metaphors with Freud's concepts of death instinct and protective shield, we could say that the death instinct is the only instinct there is, but that it has two indivisible aspects. One is Eros, the movement towards undifferentiation and absorption, and the other is Thanatos, the movement towards distinctness and expulsion, the one which produces the founding "no" necessary for any undertaking. As for the protective shield, we can define it as a semiotic envelope made up of word-things mounted on the framework of the objection to their destruction.[4] If this is so, whatever cannot be named is potentially traumatic. If something cannot be designated and described, it has no existence. Such a thing, whose existence is prevented, always crops up unexpectedly, causing the subject to fall apart, to disintegrate.

The subject is the psychosomatic being whose existence is rooted in the double trace of death which was erased in the double paradoxical movement of absorption-expulsion. The subject of whom we speak is divided between incestuous attraction and restraint (Lacan's symbolic cut). Without the trace of death, the subject has trouble living. To put it another way, the subject, this entity contained within a skin, is a unit in which all things in the world are represented by their affirmation or their negation. We can also compare the subject to a living cell surrounded by a membrane whose internal and external layers are polarised. Each thing in the world is represented virtually by a negative or positive polarity. When the subject has no negative knowledge of something that occurs, he loses consciousness. He might have an external, "positive" knowledge of something, but if his parent did not have a countervailing experience of this thing, the subject's positive knowledge has no value and cannot keep him together.

In the places where a double valence is missing, the subject is exposed and, in order to survive, must create a makeshift substitute for the missing negative. In an instant—the subject is always born in an instant—the person faced with a gap in his psychosomatic envelope builds himself a paradoxical crutch, at his own expense. Thus, we have replaced Freud's ontological system of drives with a design characterised by a paradoxical potential roughly represented by alternating movements of absorption and expulsion. Such a conceptual design should allow us to place clinical practice on a foundation other than that made possible by the theory of instincts.

The destruction of the paradoxical system causes madness, death or the birth of a new subject. When the movement of seduction-absorption, or the movement of separation-expulsion is missing, like in a context of sensory deprivation, social isolation, or solitary confinement, the subject comes apart, falls to pieces. If he does not kill himself, he invents at great cost to himself an improvised paradoxical system that manifests itself through a symptom.

Notes

1. The controversy around the question of the "origin" because the origin of representation and of the conditions of its foundation had not been discussed by the founder. Freud endowed his theoretical child with a mother whose harmoniously scanned solicitude provides ideal conditions for the creation of representations. Freud had not supposed that a problem could exist.
2. The Hebrew word connecting the invitation with the prohibition can be translated as either "and" or "but". Orthodox religious authorities, rabbis, priests, and ministers alike—guided as they are by didactic and moralising concerns—have generally translated this little word as "but". Through the centuries, introducing confusion between real and imaginary sins has served them well in maintaining their power.
3. We liken this death to that which R. M. Rilke describes in *The Book of Poverty and Death* (1903): "Not that which hangs green and without sweetness" like a fruit that will never ripen, but that "whose promise had miraculously caressed their childhood ..." God, give each one his own death, the death emerging from this life where he found love, meaning and distress. For we are but the bark and the leaf. The great death each man carries within him is the fruit at the centre of all things". Rilke, *The Book of Hours* (1905).
4. When "death" and "son" are given their proper place among these word-things, the child is protected from actual death.

CHAPTER SEVEN

Destruction of the paradoxical system: murder of the other in the self

Speak—
But don't split off No from Yes.
Give your say this meaning too:
Give it the shadow.

—Paul Celan, *Speak, You Too* (2001)

On a deserted street of a deserted city, a man and a woman are strolling with their four-year-old son. Suddenly, without a word, they decide to hide while the child is busy with a toy. When he looks up, they have disappeared. As if struck in full flight, the child does not cry, does not call out. The blood drains from his face. The trees, the birds, even the wind, are suddenly still, momentarily suspended, waiting for the child to start breathing. The parents come out of hiding.

"It was a game, you big silly.

"Look how he's shaking. He was really frightened!

"You know we wouldn't do that to you ..."

The attack just perpetrated is an almost perfect crime. The aggressors see the game only as confirmation of the child's love for them, and the child only registers the experience of coming back to life. The parents, who unknowingly enjoyed the child's terror, are anxious to come to his rescue. For his part, the child sees on their faces the pleasure they take in reanimating him. They have come back as his saviours, and he has no way to avoid considering himself the crime he just lived through, without knowing it took place.

Ever since that day, he is tormented by a guilt without cause, and acts as if he should be grateful to his parents for letting him stay alive. He bends over backwards to deserve the favour of their tyranny and to pay back the debt he has acquired towards them. He does not know that he is in the same position as the Singapore politician caricatured by Pancho in *Le Monde* on October 9, 1997. This man is portrayed between two enormous mafia thugs who are whispering in his ear: "Who can protect you better from our threats than us?"

It is impossible for him to go back to an event which has no existence, even though he lived through it. His world is left open; there is a gap in the place of the event, because this event is *something which did not take place, which has no psychic place.* But what is the world of the child? We use this term to designate the semiotic envelope which is the projection of the psychic matrix in the child. The parents contribute to the construction of this envelope by acquainting the child with various events which produce sensations. In the surprise game of hide-and-seek described above, the child is prevented from knowing a fact by the parents' passion for not knowing, which makes them swear that it was just an innocent game, certainly not intended to cause any harm. They even recount this story of fear on the deserted avenue at every family get-together, to amuse the assembled company. On these occasions, the child feels his body draw into itself and his blood drain away. In the child's semiotic envelope, associating the parent (tutelary power) with attempted murder becomes impossible. The pair of opposites, love-of-the-parent and hate-of-the-parent, was destroyed in the event on the avenue, leaving a gap in the child's protective shield.

As far as such negativist parents are concerned, nothing took place. The murder of the soul inflicted in the surprise hide-and-seek game is a nameless crime, literally unnameable and unidentifiable. The witness was reduced to silence and no one can testify. Another way to describe the consequences of this event which did not take place would be to say that the murder of the soul has killed no one. Who is dead? Nobody—as both child parents would agree. This dialogue could read as a version of that between Polyphemus and the Cyclops, who come running when they hear the cries of their fellow: "Are you the one threatened with murder?" To which Polyphemus answers: "Nobody wants to kill me."

The destruction caused by soul murder is unnameable. While God is the name of names—the name which refers to nothing other than a break in language, soul murder, on the contrary, is some thing, but a thing without existence.[1] Soul murder is a thing without name, by contrast to God, the name of names which names no thing. Rather than a name which designates nothing, what insists here is a thing which has no name. Instead of a name with no thing, of a name of names to be celebrated for itself, a thing without name persists. In this sense, soul murder is the murder of God, since it places emphasis on a thing without a name instead of insisting on the existence of the name without a thing. Where there is no shadow, God is replaced by a thing, a thing without name. The parents who hid without saying a word broke the paradoxical system of a protective shield, where all things have a shadow. Now there exists an event with no shadow and no name. The child himself is deprived of his shadow. The trace of death has been erased. He has received a deadly blow which has no psychic inscription.

What confers meaning to the usual game of "peek-a-boo ... he's gone" is the moment when the parent disappears and says that he is gone. He is invisible, but present. He is absent from the child's visual field and present in the words that announce his absence: "He's gone ... peek-a-boo". This game presents the child with the existence of that which remains unseen but speaks. The adult witnesses the child's joy at acquiring the ability conferred by speech to bring into existence a thing which is not present. This joy springs from the child's discovery that he too can accomplish an act of creation, like the act of God in the first chapter of Genesis, which we interpret as a celebration of that time in the child's life when he brings things into existence and becomes able to enjoy them when they are not present, that is, when he becomes able to think. "And God said, Let there be light: and there was light." "There is mama", "there is bread", "there is drink"—the child creates everything "there is" and makes use of it as he pleases.[2]

In the peek-a-boo game, the child tests an aspect of what we call God: the instrument of language.[3] The word does not exist, nor does God, because they are both principles of existence. God and the power that institutes the word bring into existence both what is perceived and what is invisible. They are the principles of existence but cannot be said to exist, any more than it can be said of the platinum metre at Sèvre—which served as reference to all measuring instruments before the development of atomic physics—that it measures one metre. This "metre" is the only one of which it could not be said: it measures one metre; as Wittgenstein (1968) says, it is an instrument of language. In this sense, it is not accurate to speak of the existence of God, since God is the quintessence of existence. God is the instrument of language which makes it possible to designate the generating power of the word, the power to bring into existence; just as the platinum "metre" is the instrument of language which makes it possible to speak of a metre.

The peek-a-boo game takes on a double meaning when, with his eyes closed, the child puts himself in the place of the one who is gone, and waits for the parent to say "Gone", referring to him. "Gone" and "not to see" become equivalent: he is gone, I am gone, I don't see. I don't see, therefore you don't see and I ask you to say: "He is gone." When the parent accepts the transitional role of seeing, he affirms the child's creation and the genesis of his ego. Later, the game will take the form of hide-and-seek, in which the child finds someone who is not only invisible, but silent.

In the diabolical game on the avenue, we cannot speak of "a" parent, since both parents participated in the enjoyment of the child's terror. The destruction of the paradoxical system always involves complicity between the two parents.[4] Because of this complicity in not knowing, not only at the psychic but also at the psychosomatic level, this complicity in affective non-involvement, the child's agonising experience has no witness. Soul murder is murder of the witness, the disappearance of the other in oneself.[5] No one felt it; a fortiori, no one could name it, give it existence. It exists nowhere except in the somatic archives of the child who, in certain situations, will be subject to unexplainable trembling. The soul murder committed will not acquire existence until a human being feels it and restores it to the one who was its victim.

The psychoanalyst is sometimes called upon to participate in a scene where hate is the overwhelming emotion. He is then in a paradoxical situation requiring that he feel, by empathy, hate towards the analysand. At first, he feels guilty and tries to understand his personal reasons for feeling such an undesirable emotion. Often, he suffers for a long time before he can detach himself from the scene into which the analysand draws him. For the latter, the benefit gained from this process consists in the fact that, finally, another human being will have suffered, in his body and his psyche, that which had never been embodied until then, and so had no psychosomatic site. When the psychoanalyst becomes aware that in the scene which is replayed "there is someone who hates someone", he can distance himself from the scene, read it, and put it into words, thereby giving it existence. Ferenczi was the first analyst to have seen this scene as countertransference and to incite the therapist to realise that he was being asked to bring into existence and put into words what the patient's psychosoma had experienced without registering, because there was no witness.

But what about the parents' enjoyment? This enjoyment is a sign of the expulsion of something which was persisting in them. An unnameable thing they unknowingly carried inside them was "ob-jected", thrown out, in place of the trace of death. This thing, often a far-off echo of historical events, intersecting with an event in their personal history, finds itself transposed into the child. When the transfer of events has had no site of inscription, it takes place at the level of "jouissance", the level of orgastic sensation, not recognised as such.

If origin proceeds from the erased trace of death, the subject is inscribed in the universal. Where soul murder takes place, the opposite is true: instead of death being sung/objected by the parent in whom the Siren and Circe are fused, the origin proceeds from the objection of an unnameable thing. Instead of the subject proceeding from the trace of a name designating no thing, he will evolve from a certain something without name, something which was the occasion of a bodily experience, but which acquired no psychic existence. This something is instantly constituted into the place of origin of a new subject.

For Freud, the primitive or original scene (*Urszene*) is the actual scene of intercourse between the parents, witnessed by the child—a scene on which he builds his primitive fantasies. Freud sometimes sought desperately, as in the case of the Wolf Man, to obtain the memory of such a scene from his patient.

He wanted the analysand to regain access to the image he had registered in the exquisite moment when his curiosity drove him to "see" a *scene* where the parents excluded him *and* brought him into existence at the same time: his primitive scene. Freud thought that this discovery was the necessary condition allowing the analysand to ground himself in what is universal for all humans. This scene is mainly of epistemological interest, and indicates, above all, Freud's desire to discover, as Newton did in physics, a universal law allowing no exceptions. In his enthusiasm, Freud turned the sexual into a crucial element capable of transcending all other determining factors of human fate. We believe that Man's humanity is not linked to any substance, but rather to the faculty to name all experiences to which language exposes him. This faculty depends on the parents' willingness not to defend themselves from being penetrated by all the events of the world, the good and the bad, nor from being potential hosts to all contrasting pairs and to all word-things, and first of all to their love-hate for the child. Such an opening to the "world" presupposes that the parents have a paradoxical system whose fundamental element is a name which designates no thing. This fundamental element is the instrument of language, the power of speech, which contains all words and contains itself. This power has long been called God, the "pure name" which makes it possible to name all things, including "there is".

The surprise hide-and-seek game is a founding event, but not universal in nature. The subject here is brought into an existence founded on a private act of forgetting, not into an existence common to all men. The child subjected to soul murder constructs, in an instant, a private paradoxical system which will act as his unshakable foundation. Soul murder engenders a new subject who creates otherness in a panic, either using an object—and we speak of fetishism, using a gender like his own—and we have homosexuality, using reason—and we are dealing with paranoia, or using the death of the other—and we see psychopathology.

Homosexuality allows the child to successfully escape from an invisible trap in which he was unknowingly caught. The child awakens healed of the mortal blow he does not remember, but he is transformed. Phenomenologically, the term "transformed" is not accurate, since forgetting is not an act of repression. What was forgotten has no object and no existence, while what was repressed drifts into consciousness through slips and dreams. This type of healing constitutes origins, since the object's lifetime starts at the moment when a universal or substitute paradoxical system is in place. Constructing a substitute system consists of making the opposite out of the same. When the trace of thrown-off death, the trace of the other root, has been eliminated, the child creates otherness by changing position. In the very place of the sung/thrown-off celebration of the other, of the other side of life, he can place the throwing off of the opposite sex. He will no more remember this catastrophe than a normal child remembers the gift he received of the erased trace of death from his parent.

As for the fetishist, he constructs otherness using an object, an idol, a fetish. The function of this object is to be completely reliable, unconditionally at the disposal of the one who chooses it. The fetish, heaven-sent, is a substitute for the other. Armed with this vital asset, the child no longer fears losing connection with that which is not him, since he has created the not-him himself.

When it is reason which is elevated to the rank of fetish, the resulting psychopathology is known as paranoia. Pentheus embodies it well. The hero of Euripides' "Bacchantes" refuses to take into account the invisible without seeing it. He has made objectivity his fetish and he demands that the deity submit proof of his actual existence before worshipping him. Outraged, Dionysus, the paradoxical god of both order and disorder, of the home and foreign lands, of the harvest and of festivity, puts to death all those who want to hold him hostage to reason.

For the psychopath, the death of another human being stands as a fetish. Soul murder or actual murder is required by the psychosomatic economy of the new subject. Literature abounds with examples. Don Juan is a perfect case in point for soul murder, and Polyphemus for actual murder. We believe that Don Juan is neither a homosexual who does not know it, nor the inverted figure of an Oedipus with a grievance against women, in whom he sees his mother. No, Don Juan is a delinquent. He is not bound by the law of the word because he was subjected to the murder of the other in himself. Since that day, he owes the other nothing. In fact, the other only exists to give him the spectacle of the battered, and when he takes a woman to the heights of pleasure, it is only to make her fall from the heights. Why, then, is Don Juan irresistible to women? Because he presents himself in the guise of an unconditionally loving mother, able to sing like a Siren and promising ties (through marriage) like a Circe. Don Juan fascinates all women because he is afraid of nothing and never shows signs of guilt. He represents the perfect lure of the ideal mother.

Polyphemus is the prototype of the murderous psychopathic delinquent. He is recognisable by his main physical feature: his single eye. His one-eyed vision keeps him from seeing that all things have their shadow and that God exists. When Ulysses asks him to indicate by a sign if he fears the gods—as strangers should when they first meet—Polyphemus replies arrogantly that he is not concerned with such things. Polyphemus is not subservient to the gods, he faces them without bowing before them: this is the meaning of the answer he gives Ulysses and his companions before knocking two of them to the floor of his cave and devouring them instantly, as he had said he would do. In two lines, Homer shows us three features of savagery. The Cyclops does not fear the gods, kills his host by breaking his skull, and eats him raw. One other trait, inscribed in his name, distinguishes him from Ulysses: he speaks a great deal. Etymologically, Polyphemus means "very famous" or one who "speaks much". Polyphemus says everything he thinks and everything he intends to do. Like all those who have cheated death, like Hitler, he does not hide his intentions and his plans. In this way, he misleads all those who are not psychopaths, and for whom it is inconceivable that a criminal should show himself just as he is. Polyphemus-Hitler, the living dead, does not need to cheat to mislead the living, since the latter cannot identify with someone who has been made incapable of guilt. Polyphemus-Hitler draws his life from the death of others. The death of the other, coupled with his own life, forms a substitute paradox which has taken the place of the original paradox that, in his case, was destroyed. To be a murderer is absolutely necessary to his survival, brief as that might be. Given this imperative of his internal economy, death—his own—to which he runs with eyes wide open, does not count. When the parenting context does not allow the creation of a paradoxical system, a catastrophic resolution replaces it. This substitute system becomes the foundation of a *new subject*. And this new foundation, built at the expense of sexual non-determination in some cases, or of the indeterminate play between the visible and the invisible in other cases, is not negotiable. The values which constitute it cannot be converted into another currency, and can serve no other function than to act as the backbone of the being. This catastrophic recovery gives the child existence, now that he has given himself inalienable ground by making a shift he does not recall. Psychic trauma is what brings a new subject into existence. The trauma can never be remembered, since the subject was not yet born when it occurred. The subject can no more remember the trauma which engendered him than a physicist can observe an event prior to the big bang. Concretely, the trauma does not exist. As fiction, it can only be brought to life in the course of psychoanalysis or in the form of a work of art.

Notes

1. Maurice Blanchot has given the name of God a definition with which we, psychoanalysts, are in agreement:

> Far from raising us to lofty significations, all those that theology authorises, the name of God does not give place to anything that is proper to it: pure name that does not name, but is rather always to be named, the name as name, but, in that hardly a name, without nominative power, attached as if by chance to language and, thus, transmitting to it the power—a devastating one—of non-designation, that relates it to itself.
>
> God: language speaks only as the sickness of language in as much as it is fissured, burst open, separated, a failure that language retrieves immediately as its validity, its power and its health; recuperation that is its most intimate malady, of which God, name always irretrievable, but always to be named [...] seeks to cure us, a cure in itself incurable. (Blanchot, 1992)

2. Creationists, who see God as the creator of all things, do not recognise the creative power of speech. Since they believe God's intervention to be material—He created atoms, and beings—they cannot believe in the power of words.

3. Freud (1920g, p. 15) has described this fundamental movement based on his observation of his grandson, playing a game of *fort-da* (gone-there) with a spool of thread.

4. In my opinion, Daniel Paul Schreber had a mother who was able to absent herself from scenes where her son was subjected in front of her to sexual abuse disguised as an educational measure. Nothing of what the child felt while being tortured found any echo in his parents. This situation was to cause Schreber, years later, to improvise a psychic matrix in which a very distant God is connected by rays to his skull. See Chapter Thirteen.

5. In this sense, soul murder refers to a characteristic of all totalitarian regimes.

PART II

… Japanese jugglers climb on a ladder whose base is not resting on the ground, but on the raised soles of a man half lying down, so that the ladder is not leaning against a wall, but rises straight up in the air. I cannot reproduce this feat, and not only because my ladder has no soles.

—*Franz Kafka*, The Kafka Diaries (1948)

CHAPTER EIGHT

Failure of the paradoxical system (1): before the Law

> He has discovered the Archimedean principle, but has turned it against himself; evidently, it was only on this condition that he was permitted to discover it.
>
> —Franz Kafka, *The Zürau Aphorisms of*
> *Franz Kafka* (2006)

The soul murder that occurred on the deserted city street is a perfect crime. There were no witnesses and the victim has no choice but to become an accomplice, like it or not, to the crime committed against him. Such an event finds no psychic place of inscription that could testify to it, does not have the right to exist, and cannot be recognised. In certain familial configurations—as illustrated by the case of Daniel Paul Schreber[1]—the child cannot turn to either parent because they form what Melanie Klein so aptly calls a "combined parent."[2]

Kafka is the writer who describes most accurately, and in the most colourful terms, the feat that has to be performed by a person who must maintain the symptom serving as a vicarious paradoxical foundation, a foundation he himself constructed without knowing it. Kafka shows what exploits such a person has to accomplish in order to hold together the blend of positivity and negativity he himself created out of dire necessity, how such a person exhausts himself living an existence whose conditions he must simultaneously set in place.

> Before the Law stands a doorkeeper. To this doorkeeper there comes a man from the country and prays for admittance to the Law. But the doorkeeper says that he cannot grant admittance at the moment. The man thinks it over and then asks if he will be allowed in later. "It is possible," says the doorkeeper, "but not at the moment." Since the gate stands open, as usual, and the doorkeeper steps to one side, the man stops to peer through the gateway into the interior ... (Kafka, 1915, p. 3)

The year when Freud illustrated his conception of repression using a scene where a visitor who wants to break down the door is confronted by a doorkeeper determined to prevent him from doing so, Kafka was putting forth[3] the notion that closure is not a psychosomatic configuration universally acquired at birth, and that the fate of K, the hero of his book, which begins to unfold in 1913 and which seems never to reach closure, is to confront openness (Robert, 2012).[4] We see Kafka's proposition as being related to the conditions necessary for the establishment and unfolding of a normal psychic or psychosomatic process. This process finds its equivalent in Freud's parable of repression.

In Kafka's story, the doorkeeper stands aside and the man leans forward to look inside. He sees a row of open doors, each with a doorkeeper to guard it. The man changes his mind and decides to wait until he is granted permission to enter. He sits down on the stool the doorkeeper offers him, and repeats his request. Then he assails the doorkeeper with questions, tries to bribe him, in short, does everything in his power to gain entry to the law. The scene goes on until the doorkeeper, sensing that the man's death is near, closes the gate, telling him that it was the one intended only for him.

But who is the man from the country? Some commentators translate Kafka's *Mann vom Lande* by "peasant". No, this man is not a peasant, but a man from the country. He is at once an *Amoretz*, Yiddish designation of the philistine who does not study the Book and does not observe the rites; and *Am Haaretz*, in Hebrew, the man who roams the countryside and gives up his birthright to Jacob for a plate of lentils. On the one hand, the Yiddish invites us to imagine an uneducated man contrasting with the scholar studying the law, and on the other, the Hebrew places us before an endlessly complex scene where Esau gives up his birthright and his responsibilities, and opposes Jacob, the one who is wise and crafty and who, with his mother's help, escapes his fate and takes a leap, crossing the Jabock and engaging in battle with a man who does not give his name, but who gives him a new name: Israel. According to Rachi, a commentator of the Torah, Esau, the man from the country, gives up his rights because he is afraid of making mistakes in his role as leader of other men, and in the choices he would have to make as the eldest son. Afraid of sanctions and afraid to die, Esau prefers to take no responsibility and no risk, making himself as safe as possible.

But the man from the country has yet another endorsement for the role he plays "before the law". In his diary, Kafka observes that the Talmud recommends that the Jewish scholar take an *Amoretz* with him when he goes looking for a wife, because the scholar will not be able to notice on his own the things that are essential in these circumstances (1948, p. 129). On the other hand, a man from the country knows that in this situation, speech, no doubt language par excellence, cannot take the place of other languages. A man from the country knows the difference between body language and speech and, in the presence of a long, thin, black beard, a feminine *ante portas*, he knows better than to ask questions. This passage indicates that Kafka is aware of the monstrously inflated value of the word when it pretends to compensate for what is lacking in the other languages; he seems to say that his hero is not familiar with the law formulated by Goethe and taken up by Freud: "In the beginning was the action."

Or rather, he is acquainted with this law, but by default.[5] The man from the country seems to be unaware that the law cannot be external to itself, cannot apply outside its own jurisdiction. In effect, the law cannot step outside its own domain and set the rules governing admittance to this domain. The man from the country, an outlaw, has no knowledge of the law; when he should ignore the law, like Eve ignoring the injunction to eat of the fruit of the tree of knowledge of good and evil, he asks permission and repeats his request. He acts as if the law could place itself in exile and pass legislation on the conditions of access to itself. This man from the country wants assurances and, instead of acting, taking a leap—but how does one force open an open door—he enters into an administrative process and asks the doorkeeper to tell him if … later, he will obtain admittance to the law.

The commentators who read this text merely as a reflection on the foundation of rights reduce the man from the country to the citizen of a state. The law is not only natural law, man-made law, or symbolic law, but also the law of the Jewish tradition to which Kafka belongs, despite his father's half-hearted efforts at assimilation. The word "law" is the translation—no doubt incorrect, but generally accepted—of the Hebrew word *Torah* which, when heard by a German ear, brings to mind an entranceway, *das Tor*, the gate before which stands the man from the country. "Before the Law", "Before the Gate", "Before the Torah", translations equivalent to Kafka's title *Vor dem Gesetz*, are so many added "propositions". The law is equivalent to the Torah; the Torah, then, tells the tale of the man from the country, the hero of one of the stories from Genesis. The law, *Gesetz* in German, is called *Torah* in Hebrew. And given the author's multilingualism, the man from the country finds himself before the open doors of both the law and the Torah. But a Torah without closure is scandalous, since it invites any interpretation of the law and the prophets to be based on a transtextual reading. In such a reading, the key to a word might be given by a homonym or a word with the same root, and the meaning of a sequence of words might be clarified by an identical sequence found in another text. This is why closure of the corpus of the text must be made a condition of its reading. All readings of the Torah presuppose that its corpus is circumscribed. In the absence of closure, there is nothing to interpret. In the Holy Scriptures, the most minute details take on meaning, provided that the corpus is closed. Closure is the condition necessary for the comment to remain open; this axiom is implicitly admitted by all readers of the law.

Massimo Cacciari tells us that this story is a variation on a text of the Talmud, a text discussed by the commentator Origenes (1990, p. 73). In the *Philocalies*, this great theologian recounts that a Jewish scholar told him that "[T]he Book, that is, the Law, is like a big house with many rooms, where each room has a door with a key, but the key in the lock is not the right one. The keys have been mixed up. The objective of study is to put them back in order. [But] the Law is made up of a great number of words, each word contains several letters, and each letter has six thousand faces, doors, entries. And the right key has been lost. Each face of each letter is intended for a single child of Israel. Each one has a door destined only for him." Such a palace, with all its closed doors, can only make any visitor more desirous to be let in. *Openness*, on the other hand, can only exasperate him.

Thus, the man from the country is confronted with a monstrous corpus that has no closure. Commenting on such a text is impossible, because questions about content can only be asked if the text is contained precisely, that is, if the content is well defined. Closure is necessary for interpretation just as memory and forgetting are interdependent. Kafka knows this and reiterates it in a hundred different ways; the text below, taken from his diaries, is an example:

> I can swim like everyone else, but I have a better memory than they do and I have not been able to forget the time when I could not swim. Because I have not forgotten, knowing how to swim is of no use to me, and I still don't know how to swim. (1948)

Kafka's man from the country, rather than kill himself trying to open openness, will strive to put together a closing. This is the task at which he employs himself, in collusion with the doorkeeper, who helps him construct an improvised impossibility to enter, as if he did not know that before the law, *Vor dem Gesetz*, before that which is posited, *Gesetzt*, there is no law, or a different law is in effect. So he pretends that there can be only one way to reason and, since the doorkeeper will not let him in, he will just wait until he is admitted! He decides not to decide and calls this false decision "waiting". He also pretends not to know that the doorkeeper is not there to grant him permission for anything, but to confront him before a closed door. He pretends to convince himself that there is a forbidding doorkeeper in order to ignore the fact that the door is open.

Kafka's "proposition" makes the man from the country, as well as Gregor Samsa, K., Joseph K. and Georg Bendemann, his pseudonyms, heroic spokesmen for those who wish to appeal Freud's decision to foreclose the question of the origin of the psychic process. Kafka is asking that the debate on the question of the origin be reopened, and that the decision establishing that closure is universally given be annulled. Kafka speaks for all our patients who try to make us aware that closure depends on the subjective conditions the child is given at birth. Kafka makes a plea for the question of closure to be subjected to transference.

Notes

1. Appeal Court judge made famous by the publication of his *Memoirs of my Nervous Illness*, on which Freud based his analysis of paranoia, in Freud (2002); see Chapter Thirteen.

2. We believe that Daniel Paul Schreber had such a monstrous parent: a mother connected to her mad husband by a psychotic bond, who felt nothing less and nothing other than the father's own sensations when the latter inflicted on his son the pedagogical measures that constituted sexual abuse. The mother was *in-different*, that is, had the same affect and the same thoughts as her husband, Dr Moritz Schreber. See below.

3. Kafka truly "proposes", in as much as "proposition" is a possible reading of *Vor dem Gesetz*, generally translated as "Before the Law". Massimo Cacciari (1990) suggests that this title be read literally, since *gesetzt* is the past participle of *setzen* (to posit). "Before the Law" then becomes that which is posited, put forth: that is "a proposition".

4. In "Introduction à la lecture de Kafka" (1999), Marthe Robert has pointed out that "The Process" is a closer translation of *"Der Prozess"* than *The Trial* (1925).

5. In all his writings, Kafka presents the enigma of the beginning. Everything starts with an action, and *The Trial* (*Der Prozess*) opens with an action. "Before the Law" is a segment taken from *The Trial*, the endless novel Kafka started to write in 1913, after "The Judgment", dedicated to his fiancée. After "The Judgment", *The Trial* can begin. But *Urteil*, translated by "The Judgment", also means "original score", just as *Prozess* also means "process", so that we could say: after the original separation, the process can begin.

CHAPTER NINE

Failure of the paradoxical system (2): The Silence of the Sirens and Josephine the Singer

It is dreadful to have another person's life attached to one's own, like carrying a bomb which one cannot let go of without committing a crime.

—Marcel Proust, *The Prisoner* (1923)

Kafka's journal contains an alternative version of the story of the Sirens, that the editor of his posthumous work chose to call "The Silence of the Sirens" (1931c). In this story, Ulysses is no longer the captain who has his sailors' ears filled with wax, but rather a solitary sailor who plugs his own ears with wax in order not to hear the fatal song.

To protect himself from the Sirens, Ulysses stopped his ears with wax and had himself bound to the mast of his ship. Naturally any and every traveller before him could have done the same, except those whom the Sirens allured even from a greater distance; but it was known to all the world that such things were of no help whatever. The song of the Sirens could pierce through everything, and the longing of those they seduced would have broken stronger

73

bonds than chains and masts. But Ulysses did not think of that. He trusted absolutely to his handful of wax and his fathom of chain, and in innocent elation over his little stratagem sailed out to meet the Sirens.

Before our eyes, Ulysses constructs an improvised paradoxical system in order to face the deadly danger. He knows that it does no good to stop his ears with wax—the whole world knows it—but he does not think of it. He acts *as if* this stratagem is useful and places all his trust in the little "childish" measures at his disposal: a handful of wax and a fathom of chains. They will help him pretend to be protected against the fatal weapon of these Sirens—much more terrible than that of Homer's Sirens—their silence. ... "And when Ulysses approached them, the potent song mistresses actually did not sing ..."

What protection is there against singers who do not sing?

> ... though admittedly such a thing has never happened, still it is conceivable that someone might possibly have escaped from their singing, but from their silence certainly never. Against the feeling of having triumphed over them by one's own strength, and the consequent *exaltation* that bears down everything before it, no earthly powers could have remained intact (emphasis added).

Of course, Ulysses will survive this trial, but at what cost? Or rather, what price has he already paid to survive such a perilous confrontation? The normal child is one for whom a Siren has sung, placed her faith and her hope in him, and given him her love, and in whom he could in turn place his faith. These three "virtues"—that Christianity calls theological and prescribes to the believer—give the child the ability to face crises, accidents, and losses. This child draws his confidence from the quality of the faith and love bestowed on him when he was attached to the mast. In this context, "attached to the mast" is a metaphor illustrating the fact that the periods of incitation to which the child is subjected are clearly demarcated periods. Their succession constitutes a paradoxical system of attraction *and* restraint, where restraint is represented by the silent caesura between periods of sensory solicitation. In these conditions, where continuity and discontinuity alternate, the child's ego is forged, fortified, and acquires a sense of supreme singularity.

But when the parent is absorbed in another object, an unknown pain, the child does not experience rhythmic resolution and is subjected to "suspension points" instead of clear scansion. In Goya's painting *El Pelele*, young women are making a mannequin leap in the air and onto a sheet they hold by its four corners. This apparently harmless bucolic scene recalls others, much less harmless. We are thinking in particular of the "trick", a cruel game seen at country fairs in France, in which a victim is thrown up in the air repeatedly, making the crowd hilarious with laughter. A mother who does not know she is preoccupied with an object other than the child betrays the unconscious effort she is making not to recognise him by caressing, praising, reproaching, and protesting out of tune. This chaotic attention can be compared to the "trick". The child who never experiences caesuras and is given only points of suspension instead is like a victim of the "trick".

In fact, his mother, like Kafka's Sirens, is unaware that she no longer wants to seduce. "They no longer had any desire to allure, all that they wanted was to hold as long as they could the radiance that fell from Ulysses' great eyes." They did not want to allure, but did not know it, because had they been aware of it, they would have vanished on the spot. But they stayed, protected from their own attitude by the very one who was its object. For Ulysses, in fact, helps them maintain the illusion of their seduction. He continues on his way proudly, and his exaltation confirms their certainty that they are irresistible singers. Ulysses places all his cunning at the service of their "song", allowing them to make believe that they have given him a paradoxical system of seduction *and* restraint, when in fact they were only making a show of seduction without restraint.

> For a fleeting moment he saw their throats rising and falling, their breasts lifting, their eyes filled with tears, their lips half-parted, but believed that these were accompaniments to the airs which died unheard around him.
>
> Soon, however, all this faded from his sight as he fixed his gaze on the distance, the Sirens literally vanished before his resolution, and at the very moment when they were nearest to him he knew of them no longer. But they—lovelier than ever—stretched their necks and turned, let their cold hair flutter free in the wind, and forgetting everything clung with their claws to the rocks. They no longer

had any desire to allure, all that they wanted was to hold as long as
they could the radiance that fell from Ulysses' great eyes.

The Sirens, who no longer want to seduce, give an endless show of
seduction. Here, Kafka puts this pretence of seduction on trial, and
implies that a Siren who makes a show of seduction no longer wishes to
seduce, and inversely, that a Siren who wants to seduce does not make
a show of it, but simply sings. In fact, in the *Odyssey*, Ulysses does not
see the Sirens, he only hears them sing.[1]

Kafka's Ulysses, deprived of this founding song, has to build himself a vicarious paradoxical system. When he pretends to see a desire
to allure in the show invented to make up for the absence of song, *and*
when he punctuates this falsely seductive sequence by deliberately
fixing his gaze on the horizon so as to "literally" (*förmlich*) make the
Sirens disappear, he sets up such a system.[2] In this way, Ulysses actively
changes the content of the message the Sirens are sending him. He pretends to see the signs of their love in this message, and transforms their
paralysed charm into the sign of a sound sequence he pretends to hear
before punctuating it himself by turning away his gaze. This is how
he constructs a makeshift paradoxical system out of nothing, since he
invents both the melody *and* the punctuation, and since he makes *himself* the copula which ties them together. By the end of the trial, thanks
to his cunning, Ulysses has built an ersatz paradoxical system for which
he will have to remain responsible.[3]

In "Josephine the Singer, or The Mouse Folk" (1924), Kafka continues
to develop the theme of "The Silence of the Sirens". Josephine the Singer
reigns over the mouse folk. She holds them in her spell with her singing. The immense charm produced by her singing is difficult to explain
because, in fact, her singing is closer to piping. To be completely honest,
it is not singing. This does not at all mean an absence of singing—no,
it is really a case of "not singing". Josephine pipes. But, as everyone
knows, in the world of the mouse folk everyone pipes. And Josephine
pipes just like everyone else. Maybe even less well than an ordinary
country bumpkin. Anyone honest enough to admit this could say that
"Josephine's alleged vocal skill might be disproved …" But then, the
mystery of her great success would be harder to understand. To try to
understand it, it is necessary "not only to hear but to see her". What
makes Josephine different from an ordinary piper is the great emotional
display that accompanies her singing, as she stands "arms spread wide

and head thrown back". But the spell she casts is no doubt related to the impression of fragility she gives everyone who sees her. Frail and trembling, Josephine so exerts herself with her singing that her audience feels "… as if … a cold breath blowing upon her might kill her."

In some situations, Josephine's attitude could make one think that she expects every single person to lay down his life for her, and anyone who thinks this is not far wrong. Thus, Josephine, who is the cause of all things—this too is part of her character—can sometimes attract the enemy with her piping. As a result, when the people are gathered around her in these times of danger, many of them actually lose their lives. But Josephine, who believes she is protecting the people, cannot think about this. In fact, the people not only protect themselves, but they protect Josephine, and even protect her from the awareness of the protection they offer her. The people accept this tyranny with forbearance because they know that Josephine is blinded by pride. Josephine's portrait would not be complete if we did not describe the way "[she] … half dies in sheer wonderment at the sound she is producing and after such a swooning swells her performance to new and more incredible heights …"

What effect does this attitude have on the mouse folk? If we read this text as a letter to the mother, like Kafka's letter to the father, Josephine stands for the mother, while the mouse folk stand for the child. But a very particular child, since the main attribute of the mouse folk is that they have no childhood. In this world, the children cannot take the time to be children. They cannot have a real childhood because a child of the mouse folk "must look after itself just like an adult". Josephine's children have no freedom, no protection, no right to be carefree. Everything they do must make sense, even their games. Every one of these children must be "trans-parent". Josephine did not make this play on words herself, but if someone had dared to make it in her presence, no one would have thought of laughing, because "… one does not laugh at what is entrusted to one's care; to laugh would be a breach of duty." In fact, "[T]he utmost malice which the most malicious … can wreak on [her] is to say now and then: The sight of Josephine is enough to make one stop laughing." Although among the mouse folk "laughter for its own sake is never far …", no one laughs at Josephine. And so, her children have no childhood, with the result that "… a kind of unexpected, ineradicable childishness pervades [this] people …" This childishness stays with them all their lives, and Josephine profits from it. Moreover, these children who had no childhood are not only childish, but also "… prematurely old: childhood and old age come upon [them] not as upon others." They become adults instantly, with no intervening adolescence. This could explain, at least in part, why they have no musical sense. They are too old for music and content themselves with piping.

Josephine's children have endured many hardships and understand that she will always dictate their sensations. They know that she is above the law, that she is never unsure of herself, and that she will not give up any of her certainties because they are a matter of life and death. They know she wants to be admired as the most sublime singer, and they continue on their way like Ulysses in "The Silence of the Sirens".

In Sophocles' tragedy, the paradoxical system consists of Oedipus' double submission to the mundane and the divine. The crisis into which the hero is flung will give rise to a new Oedipus whose "circumstances in no way resemble the initial situation". In the *Odyssey*, Ulysses is irresistibly seduced by the song of the Sirens, and just as strongly held tied to the mast by Euriloc. For each of these heroes, the key element is the copula tying together the two forces that pull him apart. Oedipus is monstrous *and* virtuous, he transgresses *and* respects the law, he is guilty *and* not guilty, just as Ulysses is attracted *and* restrained. Both Oedipus' and Ulysses' circumstances illustrate those of a normal child immersed in a system of potentials.

When the system fails, in order to survive, the child must compensate for the loss of potential and invent, at great cost to himself, a substitute paradoxical system, a symptom. Kafka describes this process and draws the portrait of those who vanquish death using their own devices, and consequently find themselves exiled to a strange land. Alone, they cannot relive an experience whose resurgence would annihilate them, because the event where the child was close to death was not experienced. No one can bring back to life the person he was before this event. But if he consents to be different, he will find his place among men. He could, for instance, tell this story, accompanied by a stylistic device like the one Kafka so cleverly uses at the start of "The Silence of the Sirens": "… such a thing has never happened, still it is conceivable." He could become a writer, an artist, or a psychoanalyst. Initiated like Tiresias, from the place where he resides he will create links of his making with the community of men, and will recognise his brothers—those who, like him, had to construct and maintain on their own a vicarious paradoxical system.

Notes

1. The song is the paradigm of the seduction to live because song breathes and in it continuity and discontinuity are inextricably combined. The song alternates notes and pauses, expiration and inspiration. The song is a paradoxical system as fundamental as the breathing it sublimates. Rilke pays homage to breathing in the second part of his *Sonnets to Orpheus*:

> Breathing, you invisible poem!
> World-space constantly in pure
> interchange with our own being. Counterpoise,
> wherein I rhythmically happen.
> Solitary wave,
> whose gradual sea I am;
> most sparing, you of all possible seas,—
> winning of space.

(Rilke, 1962)

2. He literally makes the Sirens disappear: "When they were nearest to him he knew of them no longer."
3. "Perhaps he had really noticed [...] that the Sirens were silent, and held up to them and to the gods the aforementioned pretence merely as a sort of shield."

CHAPTER TEN

Absorption—expulsion: The Vulture

A cage went in search of a bird.

—Franz Kafka, *"Meditations on Sin, Suffering, Hope*
and the True Path" (1910)

A vulture was hacking at my feet. It had already torn my boots and stockings to shreds, now it was hacking at the feet themselves. Again and again it struck at them, then circled several times restlessly round me, then returned to continue its work. A gentleman passed by, looked on for a while, then asked me why I suffered the vulture. "I'm helpless," I said. "When it came and began to attack me, I of course tried to drive it away, even to strangle it, but these animals are very strong, it was about to spring at my face, but I preferred to sacrifice my feet. Now they are almost torn to bits." "Fancy letting yourself be tortured like this!" said the gentleman. "One shot and that's the end of the vulture." "Really?" I said. "And would you do that?" "With pleasure," said the gentleman, "I've only got to go home and get my gun. Could you wait another half hour?" "I'm not sure about that," said I, and stood for a moment rigid with pain. Then I said: "Do try it in any case, please." "Very

81

well," said the gentleman, "I'll be as quick as I can." During this conversation the vulture had been calmly listening, letting its eye rove between me and the gentleman. Now I realised that it had understood everything; it took wing, leaned far back to gain impetus, and then, like a javelin thrower, thrust its beak through my mouth, deep into me. Falling back, I was relieved to feel him drowning irretrievably in my blood, which was filling every depth, flooding every shore. (Kafka, 1936a, p. 441)

"The Vulture" is the story of a subterfuge, in which the predator who, at first, hacks at his victim, is suddenly engulfed inside him. Kafka's metaphor illustrates the trap in which the child finds himself when his mother—a mother not able to both repossess her son *and* expel him—suddenly has the urge to be enveloped by the child. The content becomes the container.

A mother eaten up with worry (Ferenczi, 1949, p. 225),[1] who expects the child to provide unconditional proof of the primary love she is not providing, is a predatory bird. Even while she was carrying the child in her womb, she was not enveloping, the picture developing in her psychic matrix was confused and without force. Now, she cannot let go of him and worries as soon as he is out of her sight. She cannot bear to lose sight of him because the internal image which would allow her to stay close to him when he is absent is too pale. Her dream screen is like a film exposed to an unnameable black sun. This mother, who can lose her enveloping qualities—her primary qualities—in an unexpected and untimely manner, becomes a "pretend" mother who pathetically asks to be recognised as the mother she pretends to be naturally. She expels onto the child the dissonance she cannot reduce. The child takes it into himself instantly.

The hero who seems to accept being tormented by the vulture, who is about to sacrifice another part of himself to him after having been unsuccessful in his attempts to drive him away, is suddenly delivered when the predator plunges inside him and disappears. The brutality of this gesture is a characteristic of catastrophic healing because such a subversive act wards off an end-of-the-world occurrence. This incorporation prevents the child from becoming aware of the loss of his parent. In fact, the child has not really lost the parent, since the latter is inside him, abolished as a tutelary power, but present within the child. If the child were to become aware that the parent has resigned, he would be banished from the world of mutual indebtedness. If he faced reality and admitted that the parent has refused all obligation towards him, he would become delinquent, that is, un-bound from any moral obligation. Here, the catastrophe can only be resolved in one of two ways: either the child swallows the monster and agrees to pay his own debt as well as the unpaid debt of the parent, or he erases any existing debt. He is either held back or delinquent.[2]

An "as if" parent does not accept his condition, refuses to recognise it, and demands to play the role of container and content alternately, as the mood strikes him. He acts as if he was pretending that the child's position is to remain undetermined—either exterior or interior. He demands to be recognised behind the mask of a protective, soothing, and providential parent and, unexpectedly, demands to be soothed by his immersion in the child. Incorporating such a parent creates a foundation of indecision in the child. He is not placed in a field of paradoxical forces where he is at once attracted and repelled, and can forge his singularity, a place of his own, a neutral space, an ego both open and closed. Instead, the subversion transferred to the child by the parent prevents the child from feeling he has any support. On the contrary, this subversion leaves him with the sensation of being open.

This image, the open, is crucial in Kafka's writing. He describes it ceaselessly: the gate is open,[3] the Siren's mouth is half open, Ulysses' eyes are wide-open, the vulture's eye is open, and so is the mouth of the one who will swallow him. Moreover, in German, "vulture" designates openness itself, since *Geier*, vulture, comes from the Indo-Germanic *ghi*, meaning "to open the mouth wide", a root shared by German words signifying desire, longing, yawning, and sterility. The vulture is openness.[4]

When a mother in search of a self-image repeatedly begs her child: "Tell me I am beautiful, tell me I am a good mother, tell me … who I am," the child first reacts with violent anger, and then with signs of hindrance. He feels as if his legs are cut off under him, his head feels empty and he feels detached from his body. Later, to gain time, he sacrifices his feet, no longer walks, or no longer eats, or makes no progress in school … in short, he is held back. Soon he gives up and faces a mother eager to have her image confirmed. The moment he answers the insistent questioner, he forgoes his anger and swallows his illusion, the chimera that comes rushing to be swept away with him in orgasmic rapture.

The vulture—female sphinx familiar to us in our practice—proceeds from the parent whose strategy, not clearly defined but infallible, is to seduce the child in order to make him respond to her distress and let her displace him by insinuating herself under his skin. The mother, distracted from her image and seduced by an unnameable thing, is not in possession of a "death of her own" and, like the Sirens in "The Silence of the Sirens", no longer wants to seduce. The refusal to understand her position—which she passionately defends—makes her attribute to the child the effects of the absence of response to a call she did not perceive. This is a profanation of the child's space. When the mother refuses to admit the part she plays in a state of rhythmic dissonance persisting in the child, she puts a brutal end to the indecision about the source of the excitation and decides on her own authority that this excitation is external to her and must be inherent to the child. This refusal triggers an unavoidable emotion in the one whose transitional space has been violated.

Winnicott advances the idea that the question of whether the child has created the transitional object himself or whether it was given to him is not to be formulated.

> Of the transitional object, it can be said that it is a matter of agreement between us and the baby that we will never ask the question: "Did you conceive of this or was it presented to you from without?" The important point is that no decision on this point is expected. The question is not to be formulated. (1971, p. 12)

If the child is asked if his transitional object comes from within or from without, if it is objective or subjective, real or fictitious, he can no longer play. He is condemned to the realm of truth, separated from illusion and arbitrarily declared to have positive knowledge of the thing. From that moment on, he is impeded. But impeded from what? Impeded from remembering the vital illusion that he is the creator of the object; he is chased away abruptly from the original transitional realm, where the principle of non-contradiction does not exist, where things have the right to be and not to be all at once. He is deprived of the run-up needed to jump over the life-death, fiction-truth chasm, and is led back to the place of truth, the place of death. Such an event resembles the hide-and-seek game on the deserted city street. We see it as a form of soul murder. The child is turned away from the work of creating his ego, in the sense that he is turned away from the work of achieving separation from the non-ego. The authoritarian negation of the indefinable character of the origin of the transitional object is an attack perpetrated on the paradoxical structure good-bad, subjective-objective, within-without that makes up the subject.

The good-enough mother does not give the breast, but arranges for the baby to discover and create it (Winnicott, 1971, p. 12). She lets him restore the rhythm whose interruption he called to her attention a moment ago. By doing so, she gives the child the illusion that he is the one who finds a way to repair the pain created by dissonance. She arranges for the child to take the good to himself and leave her the bad. She bears the bad and with it, discontinuity and the trace of death. Already recognised as the object of someone's affection, the child becomes the subject of his own appeasement. Now, he can face the exterior where he has placed the bad that the mother bears.

On the other hand, when what his senses tell him is not recognised, the child has an experience of non-response. This, only in a manner of speaking because, strictly speaking, non-response is not an experience. Non-response cannot constitute an experience.

> Someone else's death affects me in my identity as a responsible subject […]. This way I am affected by someone else's death is my relation to his death. It is in my relation to someone who no longer responds. (Levinas, 1993)

The child who meets with non-response is refused the acknowledgement of having been affected and, at the same time, is deprived of his virtual illusion of being the subject who repairs the dissonance. In this situation, he can be compared to the one who swallows the vulture, the creature who gives no answer. Instantly, he starts to shake with chills (Ferenczi, 1949, p. 225).[5] He has taken the death of the other into himself, prematurely. Sexual enjoyment, unrecognisable in the disguise of an attack of terror, is an emergency measure that reconstitutes a subject for the child. A new subject is put together in a panic out of an ego undergoing an intense sensation and an "I" is recreated through sexual enjoyment.

The "sexual" processes all accidents of psychic life. Advocates of trauma theory and defenders of fantasy theory have long opposed each other. The latter maintain that rape is always facilitated, even provoked by the "ideational representative" of a sexual drive in the victim. The other group considers rape an event to which someone is subjected, and nothing more. Some analysts, including me, agree that rape is an accident endured passively, but understand that enjoyment is the only means the victim has of humanising the crime to which she is subjected. Sexual enjoyment, even painful and cruel, restores a paradoxical foundation in the victim, reconstitutes a subject. In experiencing sexual enjoyment, the victim reconstructs a transitional field where an object can be at once internal and external, subjective and objective, good-bad and, above all, active-passive. A therapist who does not recognise the vital function of the enjoyment experienced by the victim of an accidental event, of a crime, denies the restorative role of the paradoxical foundation the victim puts in place in order to survive. Sexual enjoyment is a human creation in the face of aggression, not a sign of return to an animal state.[6]

Incest is an attempt to humanise devastating circumstances and be able to survive. Incest between Lot and his daughters after the destruction of Sodom is an early illustration of this point. To say that incest makes it possible to humanise soul murder is to say that the "sexual" processes what is not symbolised. In this context, the sexual is understood to be the psychosomatic function that processes all accidents of psychic life, and steps in first to erase and bring out (*aufheben*) events that have no psychic inscription, that could not be symbolised.

Early seduction of the child, be it tied to soul murder or to sexual abuse, causes the child to take death into himself prematurely. Normally, a child absorbs *and* expels radical discontinuity, the trace of death—a universal horizon common to all men, which can be celebrated in a ritual. Here, however, the death of the other can only be absorbed. It cannot be absorbed-expelled because it cannot be named, since it has no existence.[7]

In certain circumstances, a subject decides to bring into question the catastrophic healing that has harmed him, and sees a psychoanalyst. This means that he has to "dis-corporate" the dead witness that he incorporated in a panic in order to make him disappear. When the work leading to expulsion is possible and unfolds to the end, the one who was not answering becomes a "vulture". At the end of the process, he has been symbolised and given a name. Kafka's vulture resembles Edgar Allan Poe's raven, who endlessly repeats "never more", a phrase identical and true to itself, deadening and enlivening forever. This raven, says Nicolas Abraham (Abraham & Torok, 1994, p. 113) is the one who inspires the poet. The poet could not write such a text unless *the thing* that impeded him has been transformed into a raven or a vulture. This creature, while remaining a source of suffering for the poet, is also the one that gives him the greatest joy, and enchants his reader. *The thing* which once was the bad has become good *and* bad, like the fruit of the tree of knowledge, like a transitional object; the thing is finally absorbed *and* expelled, interior *and* exterior.

To do things in the right order, "The Vulture" should be read after "The Judgment" (*Das Urteil*), which means "original score" (see Chapter Twelve). Only after the poet has recounted the putting to death of the subject who, waiting for his parents' permission to cross the threshold they are trying to hide from him, after the trial of the "original score", then and only then can the poet tell the story of the absorption of the silent witness. After the intense session in which he wrote "The Judgment," and which he describes in his journal as the moment of birth of a writer, Kafka can describe an absorption fantasy. The paradox of "The Vulture" consists in the fact that telling the story of the monster's absorption testifies to his expulsion.

Notes

1. Sandor Ferenczi (1949) speaks of the "terrorism of suffering".
2. A sexual reading of this text is both accurate and inaccurate. But it would be disastrous to apply it. Of course, "The Vulture" can be read as a scene of *fellatio* by a phallic mother. In that case, the scene would have an incestuous culmination. But we feel it is more appropriate to interpret the "relief" of the hero as a desperate attempt to humanise the subversion wrought by the parent by sexualising it. Giving this construction a sexual connotation would mean blaming the patient for his attempt to humanise the subversion to which he was subjected. Interpreting it as residual sexual perversion would mean accusing the patient of having written a play under threat of death. The phantasm of fellatio indicating the moment of incorporation when the person escapes psychic death surely reminds any psychoanalyst of Freud's text on Leonardo da Vinci (1910c).
3. In Kafka's work, doors that do not function as they should abound. The following is a quote from *The Kafka Diaries* (1948):

   > There is a strange door in his apartment: once it is bolted, it can no longer be opened without taking it off its hinges. Therefore, he never closes it; and to prevent it from closing, he places a wooden board in the space that leaves the door half-open.

This, of course, deprives him of the comfort of his apartment. Although his neighbours are certainly trustworthy, he has to carry his valuables with him all day long in a bag. When he is lying on the sofa in his room, it is as if he was in the hall. In summer he breathes the suffocating air of the hallway, in winter he is chilled by its icy air.

4. We should also point out that the word for "vulture" in Hebrew (a language not to be overlooked when speaking of Kafka, who made a serious study of it in the last years of his life) is RaCHaM. The dictionary definition specifies that the bird owes its name to the love it shows its offspring. In fact, RaCHaM means matrix, uterus, breast; and the verb RaCHaM means to love, to have compassion, and to be full of empathy.

5. Sandor Ferenczi (1949) speaks of *Erschütterung*.

6. The humanising sexualisation of the crime by the victim does not, of course, negate the criminal's legal responsibility.

7. This is absorption applying to incorporation, described by Abraham and Torok (1994) as absorption-expulsion attributed to introjection.

CHAPTER ELEVEN

The vicarious system of the man-from-the-country

Much encouragement is needed.

—Sandor Ferenczi, *"Clinical Diary"* (1988)

In the beginning, the cry of expulsion of a normal mother is a caesura that tears through the chaos and creates time-space. This cry owes its force to an objection to death, the death to which it pays tribute. The initial caesura of this first "no" gives a foundation and a meaning to subsequent songs and signs of love (Freud, 1925h, p. 239).[1]

But this first objection is never pure; absolute purity only exists in the figure of the Oedipus complex: the set of hypotheses and axioms that define the case of a theoretical child whose parent placed the objection to death in him before taking it back on himself. Such a child would have a perfect capacity for symbolisation and self-reflection, a capacity free of all artefacts.

Between the parent and his death, imprinted on the *psyche-soma*, lurk the shadows of losses unmourned, of offences and injustices left unmended, of all the non-symbolised events that his history carries. These imprints are made of character traits, of tendencies that distinguish individuals, clans, groups of people. They are fixed and have become insensitive, like Kafka's tired wounds in "Prometheus" (1931b, p. 432), a short text that gives some variations on the myth.

> According to the third [variation] his treachery was forgotten in the course of thousands of years, forgotten by the gods, the eagles, forgotten by himself.
> According to the fourth, everyone grew weary of the meaningless affair. The gods grew weary, the eagles grew weary, the wound closed wearily.

I do not intend to deal with the vast field that could be called normal psychopathology. My purpose is to sketch a revised version of psychopathology *per se*, from a particular point of view.

This field shapes itself according to whether or not the subject has been the victim of an attempt on the life of the Other-in-the-self. I capitalise "other" to let the concept include such apparently varied notions as discontinuity, trace of death, conditions of sense, context, ritual, that is, everything external to meaning, everything radically other than meaning, but which organises and conditions it. Everything Nicolas Abraham calls the absent Other, and Lacan, the symbolic. Soulmurder destroys this Other. Psychopathological syndromes fall either into the category of hysteria or paranoia. Hysteria includes all situations in which soul murder did not take place, while paranoia defines situations where the Other was violently ill-treated.

We agree with Freud's 1892 definition of hysteria: "The hysteric suffers from reminiscences." He suffers from a refusal of translation Freud calls repression. An event took place and was duly inscribed. But it is forbidden to translate it, or it is translated into a different language. This event is prohibited from entering consciousness, but is represented there through slips of the tongue, dreams, and actions that are signs of what is repressed, and seem incomprehensible at first sight. In some situations, all of which have some connection with the forbidden thing, the child is defenceless, surprised, disconcerted. In the semiotic envelope woven by the parent for the child, a space appears where meaning panics. When this happens, the child invents a symptom that repairs his protective shield and gives the ego a container. Freud maintained that this symptom satisfied both the desire and the defence; therefore, without saying it in so many words, he was describing an actual paradoxical system in which the satisfaction of a sexual desire is linked to its "inter-diction". Such a symptom is naturally assimilated into the Oedipus complex because the parent, unable to translate the forbidden thing, creates, at this location in the semiotic envelope he offers the child, a space of wordless communication easy to read as a sign of incestuous attraction by a reader who adopts Freud's perspective on the theory of instincts.

The situation applying to paranoia is very different. Here, an event is unnameable, not because its conscious representation is forbidden, but because it has no psychic location. The event is out-of-thought/ unthinkable, instead of merely untranslatable. An event that has taken place does not have a place in the psychic matrix the parent offers the child as the mirror in which to see his reflection. This event "which did not take place", which has no psychic existence in the parent, although it organises his *psyche-soma*, persists in the parent's life. Instead of throwing off the trace of his own death, the parent will throw off onto the child the trace of this event that did not take place.

Often, such a parent strives to counter the attempts made by the child to create an original vicarious paradox. This is the situation illustrated by Gregor Samsa's parents in *The Metamorphosis* (1915), where Kafka portrays parents who refuse their child the singular mutation— into vermin[2]—that he has found in order to survive. By doing so, the parents refuse the child access to a prehistory, acting as if his birth came about from the mere meeting of chromosomes. Consequently, the child is accountable for his origin and soon after, for his choices and symptoms. He moves about with difficulty in a structure set up in a way that makes it possible for everything to turn against him at any moment. He is like the guest who falls into the trap set by a host who suggests that he should invite himself: "Come to dinner whenever you like." But a host who refuses to take the responsibility that should be his can turn on his guest at any moment, reminding him that he invited himself. The child whose parent takes no responsibility is handicapped by guilt without an object and invents an original fiction in which a guilty party indefinitely awaits the judgment of a court that never convenes.

When a child is not conceived in both biology and fiction, when his life starts under the sign of "no history", when he is not inscribed in an original fiction, or when this fiction in invalidated by the fact that his parents transferred to him the bodily archives of a crime perpetrated against them, he must give himself an original fiction. And the giving of this gift always happens in a flash, is as swift as Cupid's arrow. In a flash, a new subject is born.[3] He either gives himself a new ego, or he amputates his "I". The flash of lightning can crystallise the love of the "I" for a new ego—as is the case for homosexuals; or it crystallises the ties of a new "I"—that has given up all action—with an ego that will not sacrifice anything and adopts, in a panic, a conservative attitude. This is the case of the man from the country who strives to cover up the attempted murder whose object he does not know he was, and harnesses himself to the waterwheel that ensures the survival of an "I" amputated of its ability to act. The "I" sees everything but is nailed to the spot as if it had been forced to choose, once and for all, between understanding and taking action. In the meantime … he kills time, whose paradoxical parameters have not been revealed to him.

The story "Before the Law" best illustrates the situation of a person who strives to build himself, from scratch, a vicarious paradoxical system. The man from the country and the guardian of the law are indissociable and are to be taken as one. In the following transcription of the story, "I" refers to the man from the country who, from all appearances, is trying to enter the law; the word "Ego" designates the doorkeeper who attempts to dissuade him.

> Before the Law stands the Ego. To this Ego there comes the I and prays for admittance to the Law. But the Ego says that he cannot grant admittance at the moment. The I thinks it over and then asks if he will be allowed in later. "It is possible," says the Ego, "but not at the moment." Since the gate stands open, as usual, and the Ego steps to one side, the I stoops to peer through the gateway into the interior. Observing that, the Ego laughs and says: "If you are so drawn to it, just try to go in despite my veto. But take note: I am powerful. And I am only the least of the Egos. From hall to hall there is one Ego after another, each more powerful than the last. The third Ego is already so terrible that even I cannot bear to look at him." These are difficulties the I has not expected; the Law, he thinks, should surely be accessible at all times and to everyone, but as he now takes a closer look at the Ego in his fur coat, with his big sharp nose and long, thin, black Tartar beard, he decides that it is better to wait until he gets permission to enter. The Ego gives him a stool and lets him sit down at one side of the door. There he sits for days and years. He makes many attempts to be admitted, and wearies the Ego by his importunity. The Ego frequently has little

interviews with him, asking him questions about his home and many other things, but the questions are put indifferently, as great lords put them, and always finish with the statement that he cannot be let in yet. The I, who has furnished himself with many things for his journey, sacrifices all he has, however valuable, to bribe the Ego. The Ego accepts everything, but always with the remark: "I am only taking it to keep you from thinking you have omitted anything." During these many years the I fixes his attention almost continuously on the Ego. He forgets the other Egos, and this first one seems to him the sole obstacle preventing access to the Law. He curses his bad luck, in his early years boldly and loudly; later, as he grows old, he only grumbles to himself. He becomes childish, and since in his yearlong contemplation of the Ego he has come to know even the fleas in his fur collar, he begs the fleas as well to help him and to change the Ego's mind. At length his eyesight begins to fail, and he does not know whether the world is really darker or whether his eyes are only deceiving him. Yet in his darkness he is now aware of a radiance that streams inextinguishably from the gateway of the Law. Now he has not very long to live. Before he dies, all his experiences in these long years gather themselves in his head to one point, a question he has not yet asked the Ego. He waves him nearer, since he can no longer raise his stiffening body. The Ego has to bend low toward him, for the difference in height between them has altered much to the I's disadvantage. "What do you want to know now?" asks the Ego. "You are insatiable." "Everyone strives to reach the Law," says the I, "so how does it happen that for all these many years no one but myself has ever begged for admittance?" The Ego recognises that the I has reached his end, and, to let his failing senses catch the words, roars in his ear: "No one else could ever be admitted here, since this gate was made only for you. I am now going to shut it." (Kafka, 1916, p. 3)

Kafka's hero is striving to give himself a substitute for the trace of death, but this vicarious paradox, which should have been the foundation of his existence, is now constructed at its expense. The hero strives to live and not to live, and this occupation, like the payment of an infinite debt, leaves him no respite. When death is finally near, he is freed from the obligation of making its trace exist and he can join humankind at last … through the door of dying.

Literature gives us other figures that enter the human realm by the same door. One of them, Edmond Rostand's Cyrano, can only obtain Roxane's love when he is dying. Before that, he lends his voice to his enemy, the handsome Christian, and he hides the giant nose (*nez géant*) that reveals his *nothingness* (*néant*) the sign of soul murder he wears in the middle of his face. Don Juan illustrates the same phenomenon, but in a different way. Contrary to Cyrano or to Kafka's hero, Don Juan is not trying to hide behind a borrowed persona, like Cyrano. All he expects of others is that they lend themselves to the repetition of the crime perpetrated against him, murder of the other in the self. He is taken up, body and soul, with the actions necessary to carry this out. His frenzy is related to the fact that if he ever abandoned himself to a woman, she would discover that his *psyche* reflects no image. Therefore, Don Juan is always on his guard, and cannot let the other get hold of his image. Even when he is dying, he cannot entrust his image to the other, because he is convinced he does not have one.

When a person has changed his ego, as it were, and emerges as a new subject, the catastrophe has been given resolution. This is most often true of the "Zeus" who, in a flash of lightning, creates the homosexual's solution. One morning he wakes up different, but his new foundation is a forgotten death threat. This post-traumatic origin brings about relational distortions evidenced by the disastrous results achieved by his efforts to maintain "normal" ties with his family. In retrospect, he will see these efforts as desperate attempts to act as if nothing has happened.

When the man from the country, the one who has cut himself off from his ability to act—the one who changed his "I"—decides to undergo psychoanalysis, he is likely to find that his analyst is as unable to make a leap as he is himself. The misunderstanding can last for a very long time and can even bring the analysand the short-lived satisfaction of being able to blame the analyst for the failure of the treatment. But after a time the man from the country feels that his internal and external resources allow him to bring his vicarious foundations into question. He then undertakes a formidable battle in which he attacks himself, that is, the new subject he invented for himself. The enterprise is marked by withdrawals, interruptions, returns. It is a bumpy road, a perilous journey, and trying, because the analysand runs the risk of losing his present coherence before he can reconstruct himself.

He baulks at losing the protection of his murderers who stop at nothing in their efforts to dissuade him from continuing on this journey. His parents, his friends, his lovers, even his children speak for him, flatter him, sing his praises, use blackmail, in short, set all manner of traps. They propose discussions, draw him into arguments, use logic—all of these being nothing but cleverly disguised traps. These endless arguments and discussions are all occasions where he is invited to find himself on familiar ground, in the universe he has inhabited since his new origin. Kafka writes in his "Diaries" that dialogue is one of Evil's most effective means of seduction. We interpret this aphorism to refer to those situations where the ego is inextricably bound to itself through the efforts of those who feed on its destruction by maintaining an endless dialogue with it.

A psychoanalyst who understands how difficult it is for the new subject to question the means of survival he discovered as a child in a critical moment can assist a person who wants to bring into question the state of deferral in which he lives. Long ago, the child put in place an economy of survival. This internal economy determined that there is nothing left to determine. Today, the person is seeking to give up these conservative parameters. But abandoning such a safe position seems deadly dangerous. Only those who have gone through this experience know how painful it is to let go of an ego constructed in a panic, to attack the bastion one has built oneself. A raging battle goes on between the one who wants to wake up and wake up everyone asleep in the castle of Sleeping Beauty, and the one who wants to stay still and remain loyal to a shell, to the image he has been showing since the new origin which is his foundation. This shell that might be hated, nevertheless gives the new subject definition, makes him feel at home. Mended by his symptom, the subject created the conditions needed to survive, and chose friends and lovers who accepted his foundation because it reinforced their own.

When those who reinforce his vicarious paradox are immovable, either because they are dead or because they are not ready to move, and the new subject finds himself in favourable conditions, he might attempt to make an escape on his own. But the land where human beings speak to each other, disagree, negotiate, reanimate the past and forget it again, is unfamiliar to him. Everything seems foreign to him, and he feels endangered because in this land he has no way of getting his bearings. This is a fearful time because he sometimes has sensations close to those that drove him to swallow the unnameable in order to escape death. Ever since the unremembered day when he became a "bridge" for himself, he no longer knows how to lean on the other, he does not know that a plea can be addressed to him and an answer expected.

When the psychoanalyst consents to play a role in the scenes the analysand proposes, and when the former recognises that his participation is active, the characters come to life and the play is brought into the present (Davoine, 2012; Searles, 1970).[4]

An analyst who has been through the same trial can show compassion and give the analysand the encouragement he needs to be able to delve into the deepest corners of his own being and of nothingness.

Notes

1. In his article "Negation" (1925h), Freud suggests that "yes" is the substitute for Eros, and "no" the successor of forces of destruction. In "Le non et la position de l'objet" (1971, p. 117 ff.), J. -F. Lyotard has remarked very pertinently that the successor has a very different value than the substitute. To say that the "no" inherits a negative charge while the "yes" is only a substitute for positive charges is the same as saying that a single life-and-death instinct governs the economy of psychic life. The corollary to this hypothesis would be that the origin starts with a "no", just as the caesura retroactively organises the rhythmic sequence.
2. Kafka uses the German term *Ungeziefer* which comes from the High German *Zepar*, meaning "scapegoat": *Wörterbuch Duden*.
3. No doubt the technique of electroshock, invented in 1938 to treat melancholia, is the scientistic objectification of the intuition that fundamental forgetting, the necessary condition for the birth of the *subject*, always appears to be the effect of lightning.
4. This attitude, fundamental to Ferenczi's therapy, was taken up, renewed and developed by Harold Searles in *Countertransference and Related Subjects*, 1970), as well as by Françoise Davoine (2012) in *Wittgenstein's Folly*.

CHAPTER TWELVE

The paradox of the birth of the artist: The Judgment

"[…] because the story ["The Judgment"] came out of me like a real birth, covered with filth and slime, and only I have the hand that can reach to the body itself and the strength of desire to do so."

—Franz Kafka, *The Kafka Diaries* (1948)

"In a great fire in which fancies … perish and rise up again" Kafka found the words to write his masterpiece, "The Judgment". "With … a complete opening out of the body and the soul", he gave birth to the writer who would be one of the great artists of his century and who, for certain Jewish thinkers, represents a renewal of the figure of the prophet.

This story, "The Judgment", I wrote at one sitting during the night of the 22nd–23rd (September 1912), from ten o'clock at night to six o'clock in the morning. I was hardly able to pull my legs out from under the desk, they had got so stiff from sitting.

The next day, Kafka knew he had become a writer and that nothing could make him deviate from the path that had opened before him that night.

"The fearful strain and joy, how the story developed before me, as if I were advancing over water" (Kafka, 1948, p. 212).

Ten months later, on June 21, 1913, he writes in his diary that writing is his destiny:

> The tremendous world I have in my head. But how free myself and free it without being torn to pieces. And a thousand times rather be torn to pieces than retain it in me or bury it. That, indeed, is why I am here, that is quite clear to me.

Like a tragedy, "The Judgment" (Kafka, 1913, p. 77) is constructed in two parts, around the crucial catastrophe that plunges Georg Bendemann into the river where he rushes to carry out the sentence pronounced by his father. In the first part, Georg, "on a Sunday morning in the very height of spring", is reflecting on the fate of a friend to whom he has just written to announce his engagement. This friend, exiled, alone, and in poor health, has "obviously run off the rails" by going abroad. Georg hesitated a long time before writing to him to announce the happy event, because he did not want to hurt him. But because his fiancée insisted, he decided to go ahead; now, he has just given the news to his elderly, bedridden father, who lives with him since the mother's death.

But, to the son's astonishment, the father is less than delighted. First, he goes off on a tangent: "St. Petersburg?" he asks, then he goes on to imply that he doubts such a friendship exists: "Do you really have this friend in St. Petersburg?" and finally accuses his son outright of wanting to deceive him because, he declares, the truth is that Georg has never had a friend in St. Petersburg. At first, Georg tries to create a diversion, carries his father to his bed, and waits for the right moment to broach the subject again and appeal to his father's memory.

"You begin to remember my friend, don't you?" But his father answers with a question, asking him if he is well *covered*. The son reassures him: "Don't worry, you're well covered up."

Here, after these words, Kafka introduces what Hölderlin calls an anti-rhythmic caesura, which causes time to be suspended before the story runs on to its outcome.

> "No!" cried his father, cutting short the answer, threw the covers
> [*Decke*] off with a strength that sent them all flying in a moment

and sprang erect in bed. Only one hand lightly touched the ceiling to steady him.

"You wanted to cover me up, I know, my young sprig, but I'm far from being covered up yet. And even if this is the last strength I have, it's enough for you, too much for you. Of course I know your friend. He would have been a son after my own heart. That's why you've been playing him false for all these years ... But thank goodness a father doesn't need to be taught how to see through his son. And now that you thought you'd got him down, so far down that you could set your bottom on him and he wouldn't move, then my fine son makes up his mind to get married!"

Georg stared at the bogey conjured up by his father. His friend in St. Petersburg, whom his father suddenly knew too well, touched his imagination as never before. Lost in the vastness of Russia he saw him. At the door of an empty, plundered warehouse he saw him. Among the wreckage of his showcases, the slashed remnants of his wares, the falling gas brackets, he was just barely standing up. Why did he have to go so far away? [...]

"Because she lifted up her skirts", his father began to flute, "because she lifted up her skirts like this, the nasty creature," and mimicking her he lifted his shirt so high that one could see the scar from his war wound, "because she lifted her skirts like this and this you made up to her, and in order to make free with her undisturbed you have disgraced your mother's memory, betrayed your friend, and stuck your father into bed so that he can't move. But he can move, or can't he?"

And he stood up quite unsupported and kicked his legs out. His insight made him radiant.

These words that come crashing down on Georg as if the roof was falling on his head leave him bereft of his father, his friend, his mother and his work:

"I'm still much the stronger of us two. All by myself I might have had to give way, but your mother has given me so much of her strength that I've established a fine connection with your friend and I have your customers here in my pocket!"

Georg finds himself confronted with the monstrous vision of a combined parent and understands that he is left with nothing of his own.

He also understands that his father has been watching him for years, waiting for the right moment to condemn his diabolical, "innocent child" character and finally pronounce the sentence: death by drowning.

Georg, who has now lost everything except his awareness of the father (as Kafka notes in his diary on February 11, 1913), runs down the stairs, rushes outside, climbs over the railing of the bridge and jumps into the water calling in a low voice: "Dear parents, I have always loved you, all the same."

During that night spent in a state of inner jubilation, while he was writing a story of soul murder, Kafka changed subjects. Through the act of writing, he killed a young man drowning in the black storm waves of self-hatred, a young man lost in the confusion of a fate imposed by strangers. At the same time, in "a complete opening out of the body and the soul", he gave birth to a new subject, a new I-ego agency. The young Kafka, well acquainted with the indecision of the man-from-the-country, made a clear decision. He acknowledged his difference from his family and made a leap. In a flash of lucidity, he realised that neither his father nor his mother had brought into the world a child free to invent, with them, an original score—"Das Urteil", the German title of "The Judgment", can be translated as "original score"—but rather one who had to conform to a required programme.

Six months later, Kafka told his mother, in carefully chosen words, about the certainty he acquired that night while he was writing, that he and his parents don't speak the same language. The August 15, 1913 entry in his diary describes a scene where his mother comes to tell him that she doesn't understand his refusal to write to an uncle who wishes him well. Kafka answers that he has nothing in common with this uncle, who understands nothing about him.

Annoyed, his mother answers: "So no one understands you. I suppose I am a stranger to you too, and your father as well. So we all want only what is bad for you." Franz answers: "Certainly, you are all strangers to me, we are related only by blood, but that never shows itself. Of course you don't want what is bad for me."

That night of September 22, 1912, through the act of writing Kafka killed an image of himself. Yesterday's subject, who belonged to his parents' imaginary world, was symbolically slain. After going through trials in which death is glimpsed as in an initiation ritual, he attains another world in which he has the attributes of a man. Concretely, the attributes Franz acquires do not take the form of weapons, but rather of a pen that gives him access to the community of writers. But Kafka is more than that—his friend, Max Brod, is a writer too—he is also a seer. From this point of view, "The Judgment" reads like a variation on *Oedipus Rex*, whose hero, confronted with the truth, has no choice but to leave the world. In Kafka's case, the son leaves his parents' world without a fuss. It is his own voice that praises death and objects to it. He makes the best of it, he will become a poet, the witness to murder, the herald of an original sphere in which all things have their shadows.

During his night of writing, Kafka left the country of his childhood. He exiled himself from the country of his mother and father which is, among other things, that of the wounded Jews who pursue ever faster assimilation but go to the synagogue on the Day of Atonement. No doubt that the day before—that year, Yom Kippur, the Day of Atonement, was celebrated on September 21—his father, knowing neither the Hebrew language nor the tradition, had paid no attention to the meaning of the rituals and the texts that were read. By writing "The Judgment", Kafka was reminding his father that the New Year, Rosh Hashanah, is first of all the first of the ten terrible days that lead to the Day of Atonement; and that Rosh Hashanah is above all the day of remembrance when the Jew recalls his faults, his errors, and his failings, in order to have his name entered in the Book of Life. He was also reminding him that Yom Kippur is the day when the Jew prays for the forgiveness of his sins against God, but not those committed against his neighbour, because the latter can only be forgiven by the neighbour. Most of all, Kafka instructs his father that the main theme of Yom Kippur is "covering" (see below).

Thus, "on a Sunday morning in the very height of spring", Georg asks his father to remember this friend who is ill, ruined, alone, and exiled in a foreign country. But who is this friend? We consider him to be the wounded child the father once was, the one he cannot admit dwells within him, the one he throws off onto his son. Let us note that the friend's beard does "not quite conceal the face Georg had known so well since childhood". This is the child Georg wants to protect, to take care of and to treat with the greatest consideration possible. But the father wants none of it, and divests his son of his charitable enterprise. He declares that this friend crumples up Georg's letters in one hand, while reading his (the father's) in the other, and that the friend has always been his, not Georg's. The son's ambition to maintain friendly relations with this grown, wounded, suffering child the father carries inside him deserves punishment. It would have been easier to become the unproblematic child his indivisible parents intended to make of him. The son who dares to discover the death that the father wanted to ward off by bringing him into the world, this "sickness" he wanted the birth of the son to conceal, is justly condemned to death.

This father did not give his son life unconditionally, he is not an unconditional parent, he granted his son life on the immutable condition that he become his ally in covering up the soul murder whose victim he was himself as a child. A son who refuses this alliance in covering up, who does not accept the forgetting on which fatherhood is anchored, becomes an enemy and must suffer *per contrapasso*, as Dante says, a punishment identical to the crime he is uncovering.

When Abraham stays his arm—in the sequence about Isaac's ligature, which is read at Rosh Hashanah and at Yom Kippur—he gives his son life, accepts the course of time and pays his debt to the symbolic order, to have a son who will one day cover him up. Because he sacrifices to the absent other, Abraham interrupts the monstrous natural course of events in which a powerful man slays his offspring before the latter has a chance to kill him when he becomes too weak to defend himself.[1] But there is more, and thanks to Kafka and Freud we also read in this text the instance when a father, in this case Abraham, forfeits the slaying of the child in distress, the child he once was. He chooses not to kill his son and eliminate with him the pain he unknowingly transmitted to him. Instead, he opens his heart and offers his memory as a guarantee. Reading "The Judgment" and the story of Abraham leads to the realisation that the guarantee the father can offer the child is this opening onto the pain to which he was exposed himself as a child. In his relation to the child, the father would then take responsibility for the suffering and the catastrophe inscribed in his own history. Only a father whose memory is not bankrupt, not burdened with unpaid debts, can cover his son. Not because otherwise his memory is failing, but because it is engaged elsewhere. If his debt to the absent other has not been paid, the parent cannot admit death, he cannot become involved. He expects the child to share his passion for the fetish invented at the site of something not registered in his own history, and to make the first move to be recognised before granting him recognition.

The father in "The Judgment" cannot gain access to his memory because he has not acknowledged the soul murder perpetrated upon him. Its forgetting is a founding stone of his personality. It is an event that has not taken place, and the forgetting of this assassination has made him successful, a live wire, very skilled at fulfilling his ambitions. Today, denying the crime perpetrated against him, he cannot allow his son to open the door of the virtual chamber where the injured child he once was lies asleep.

But let us return to the main theme of both "The Judgment" and atonement, the theme of covering. Chapter Sixteen of Leviticus—which is read on the Day of Atonement, describes the protocols of the slaying of the sacrificial bull and lamb. Both are sacrificed to ask God for forgiveness of the trespasses committed by the high priest and by the people. The three-consonant root K.P.R. of the word Kippur, as pointed out by Jerome Lindon in his book *Jonas*, also forms the words KaPaR, "he covered", "he forgave"; KaPeR, which designates the "coating" covering the inner and outer surfaces of Noah's Ark; as well as KaPoRet, the golden table covering the Ark of the Covenant, on and before which the high priest spreads the blood of the sacrificial animal on Yom Kippur.

The biblical book of Jonah, also read on Yom Kippur, talks about covering as well. Jonah chooses to return to the city of Tarsus, his father's dwelling place (according to a Talmudic scholar), rather than go to Nineveh to urge the inhabitants to come back into the fold. Jonah is thrown into the sea to appease the tempest. Swallowed by the monster, he travels for a time in his belly before being thrown onto the shore and then continuing on to Nineveh to carry out his mission. The Ninevites acknowledge their crimes and obtain God's forgiveness. Jonah expresses his anger at God for showing such clemency. To show Jonah what man has to endure when he is deprived of *cover*, God dries up overnight the tree he created the previous day to give Jonah shade.

Kafka has left the world without a history in which the father is busy concealing the soul murder committed against him.[2] He has thrown into the river the subject conceived for an unproblematic existence with no past and no future. Why did he choose drowning as the means to do away with this subject? No doubt, the river is the resurgence of a forgotten submerged disaster.[3]

Franz emerges from an imposed world by throwing himself into writing. In the last three sequences of the text—that lead to a birth—sexual intercourse, dwelling in a liquid milieu, and passage to a breathing state are all presented, but in reverse order.

> Out of the front door he rushed, across the roadway, driven toward the water. Already he was grasping at the railings as a starving man clutches food. He swang himself over, like the distinguished

gymnast he had once been in his youth, to his parents' pride. With weakening grip he was still holding on when he spied between the railings a motor-bus coming which would easily cover the noise of his fall, called in a voice: "Dear parents, I have always loved you, all the same," and let himself drop.

At this moment an unending stream of traffic was just going over the bridge.

The last word of this bouquet of literary fireworks is *Verkehr*. It is translated as "traffic", but it can also refer to sexual relations. Georg-Franz, who travels through air, then into water, and finally comes to intercourse, is accomplishing a birth in reverse—his own. Kafka is able to invent a support for this return to the starting point, and this support is the act of writing. This act is vital for him. He knows that writing is not life, and often makes this observation in his diary and in his letters. But writing is symbolic of the soul murder perpetrated against him, and to which he became, *nolens volens*, an accomplice. Writing is the trace of death, the trace he was not given because he was given actual death. Agreeing with Freud, Kafka could say that he has succeeded where the paranoiac fails: that he has succeeded in recognising the part he himself played in the trial of his origin.

When the parents keep enjoying their absolute embeddedness, the child with no history starts to write stories. Kafka writes them and sometime reads them to his father in the evening; his father grumbles during the reading. He probably finds his son's insistence on making up stories peculiar.

This son also knows when to invent a story. When he meets a little girl in a Steglitz park in Berlin, and learns that she is greatly distressed because she has lost her doll, he tells her (Citati, 1990):[4]

No, your doll is not lost.

- Yes, she is.
- No, she is not lost.
- How do you know?
- Because she wrote me.
- I don't believe you.
- It's true. I'll bring you the letter tomorrow.

The next day, the little girl is waiting for the letter that Kafka pulls out of his pocket.

My darling,

You might not know it, but I've been wanting to see the world for a long time. I didn't know what to do. Ask your permission? You would never have given it, and it was better to avoid an unpleasant argument. So one day I made up my mind suddenly, I caught the streetcar and hid in the side pocket of a suitcase headed for the harbor. There, I took the first ship that sailed out. I didn't know its destination, but I found out later that it was going to New York. So there I was, on my way to the New World.

You won't believe how lucky I was! I was adopted by a foreign little girl who got upset when she saw her mother, who had found me on the deck, get ready to throw me overboard. The little girl must have explained that I was the lost doll of another little girl who would be very sad to hear that I had been mistreated. We have been together ever since. I don't understand a single word she says but no matter, she sings almost as well as you do.

I will write you every day and tell you what happens. A dove comes to pick up the letters little girls want to send to their dolls back home. I will give it my letter to you.

Love and kisses.

Every day, Kafka brought a letter from the doll and read it. After a week, he wondered how to put an end to this correspondence. Dora Diamant, his companion, suggested, with typical feminine wisdom, that the doll could get married. Kafka liked the idea and, the next day, brought the last letter.

My darling,

This will be the last letter you will receive from me. Let me explain. Two days ago I wrote you that I met someone. And now, I am in love. He is a man from the country. He was very hesitant to start a relationship with me. He said that he had a secret obligation he couldn't tell me about. After a while, I came to suspect that he was looking after a very demanding animal that had a voracious appetite. Soon, I discovered that he had a small room where he spent his nights. You know how clever I am, so you can imagine that I managed to hide in his room. When I dared to look, guess what I saw?

A giant bird perched on his shoulder. As for him, he was writing …
without looking up even once. The next day I found out that this
bird is the source of all his torment and joy, and the inspiration for
every word he writes. It's a vulture.

We are going to get married and so, dear one, I think it is better
not to send you any more letters. I wish you the best of luck.

Love,
Your doll.

Notes

1. This account is that of the murder of the males of a tribe, that Kafka
   could have read in August 1912 in the third issue of *Imago*, the psychoanalytic journal; the account is signed by Freud, and Kafka could be
   thinking of *Totem and Taboo* when he writes in his diary on September
   23, 1912: "Many emotions carried along in the writing, joy, for example,
   [and] … thoughts about Freud, of course."
2. By pointing out in his "Diaries" that "Georg" has the same number of
   letters as "Franz", the author indicates that "The Judgment" is an auto-
   biographical account.
3. "Drowning" opens another subterranean door under Kafka's maternal
   territory, and leads to his tie with his grandmother who became dumb
   the day her daughter died of typhus, and who killed herself a year later
   by throwing herself into the Elbe river. Julie Kafka was three years old
   when her mother died.
4. The story is told by Pietro Citati in "Une année dans la vie de Franz
   Kafka", in *Franz Kafka, Lettres à ses parents* (1990). Pietro Citati does not
   mention his source, *ma si non è vero è ben trovato*. The contents of the two
   letters are the fruit of my imagination.

CHAPTER THIRTEEN

The resolution of a misunderstanding

He has two antagonists; the first presses him from behind, from his origins, the second bars his road ahead. He struggles with both. Actually the first supports him in his struggle with the second, for this one wants to push him forward, and in the same way the second supports him in his struggle with the first, for of course that one is driving him back. But that is only the case in theory; for it is not only the two antagonists that are present, but himself as well, and what his own intentions are who can really say?

In any case, his dream is to be left unsupervised for a moment—although for this there would have to be a night darker than any that has ever been—so that he could leave the battle front and, recognised as an experienced warrior, be made the referee in the combat between his two adversaries.

—Franz Kafka, *The Zürau Aphorisms*
of Franz Kafka (2006)

The man from the country had embarked on a psychoanalytic journey at a time in his life when, despite his protestations to the contrary, he did not want to bring into question the catastrophic healing he had brought about by force in his adolescence. In fact, as with everything he did, he took one step forward and two steps back. He spent several years this way, braced against the threat of change he had unleashed himself by undertaking this analysis, albeit unwillingly. For him, the moment of a new crisis had not yet arrived.

He became a psychoanalyst. Some of his patients made him see the benefits of the analytic experience; others brought him to the brink of a crisis that another analyst helped him overcome. After a few years of practice, when he had to assess his first analysis, he was surprised at the enormous disproportion between the great resistance to change he offered at the time, and the abundance of oedipal interpretations and judgments about his instinctual economy that his analyst provided. This surprise became the driving force behind his subsequent search.

At first, his search concerned itself with the origins of psychoanalysis. He tried to find in Freud's own life the reason for the dogmatic character psychoanalytic discourse could sometimes display. This inquiry allowed him to gain a thorough knowledge of the history of early psychoanalysis, but he soon realised that it was useless to blame Galileo for not having discovered the laws of gravity and those of relativity at the same time. He then decided to devote his time to epistemology and to clinical practice. Very quickly, he learned to be wary of Oedipus' prodigious gifts, inasmuch as this conceptual hero can be made to explain everything, especially when the notion of psychic bisexuality and the theory of instinctual duality are associated with him. His reflection led the man from the country to free metapsychology from the constraints of natural philosophy inscribed within it, particularly in the notion of drives, the theoretical counterpart to Oedipus. Now, a new space of reflection had opened and new questions could be examined.

Today, the man from the country subscribes to a metapsychology based on the association, in the *psyche-soma*, of yes and no, of death and the refusal of death. This paradox engenders the subject, the agency that presides over reflection and makes it possible to see, and to see oneself, regardless of origins.

When a child does not receive the trace of death, or when a traumatic event masks or destroys it, he must give himself the negative that was refused him or taken away. He must create a vicarious paradox in a great hurry and on his own. To fill a gap carved into the ego by an event imprinted in his body—but with no visual, auditory or memory trace—the subject sacrifices one of his relational functions for the sake of creating the missing negative. One person might give up his sexual identity, another his initiative, yet another his judgment. This production of the negative provides him with support and enables him to constitute his own reflection in the mirror of his thinking, around the blind spot of his new origin, site of his new "primal scene". A vicarious paradox has been extemporaneously substituted for the original paradox, and with it, a new regime—for instance, of sexual orientation, has been introduced. By cutting away one of his functions and giving it a negative charge, a new subject gives birth to himself. He provides the conditions for existence at his own cost. At least, this is so for those who were not obliged to sacrifice the very consistency of their ego, as is the case for the psychotic.

In the course of analysis, if the context allows it and if the psychoanalyst does not oppose it and is well disposed to it, the analysand is sometimes ready to reopen the trial of his origins and bring into question his "catastrophic healing". Such an analysand is heroic because changing subjects or attempting to recover the subject at the foundations means risking to lose everything and to dismantle defences built at great cost. When he takes this risk he is, like Oedipus, at once loyal and disloyal to himself. Loyal in that he expels the thing that acted as a screen between his birth and his death; disloyal in that he attacks the foundations of the being he had reconstituted in a flash, at the moment of his rebirth.

This perspective gives rise to a practice different than that Freud based on original repression and on an instinctual capital he assumed to be universally acquired. The dynamic of forfeiting this or that instinct, proposed to the patient by an analyst too loyal to Freud, is replaced by a dynamic of repossession of events not having had a place of inscription. The man from the country now viewed the incestuous or murderous instincts Freud attributed to every child as signs of an absence of separation between the parent and a part of the child. An incestuous relationship does not spring from some instinctual anomaly, but rather from the inherent characteristic of an object. Such an object, the shadow of an event with no psychic inscription, makes the parent and the child inseparable, bound together in love or in hate, as long as an analyst able to experience and name this event is not invited to intercede. In this context, "negative transfer" appears most often to be linked to the fact that the analysand sees superimposed on his story a theory that no longer has any value other than epistemological.

If, as Gilles Deleuze says, Faulkner writes for idiots and he himself writes for animals, Kafka writes for negationists, those who do not know that they were accomplices to a crime perpetrated against them, a crime their aggressor negates as passionately as they do. As for this book, it was written in order to attest to the fact that, following Kafka's example, anyone can let go of the ties created out of the worst, in an emergency, for the sake of survival; and to say, moreover, that a psychoanalyst can help accomplish this, provided, first of all, that he can put Oedipus in his proper place. Because Oedipus, with his admirable heuristic qualities, has all the answers; this is why he has been used for the purposes of the most outrageous popularisation of psychoanalysis, and been made to serve a form of lazy reflection that has sometimes led to a damaging and vulgar practice. Through writing, the man from the country gave himself the means to resist the seduction of the ready-made answer, and to say to himself regarding the question of the origin of the subject, that as Kafka writes in "The Test" (1936b):

"He who does not answer the questions has passed the test."

Schreber's transsexuality as catastrophic healing and method of survival after the destruction of the paradoxical system

> He has the feeling that merely by being alive he is blocking his own way. From this sense of hindrance, in turn, he deduces the proof that he is alive.
>
> —Franz Kafka, *The Zürau Aphorisms*
> *of Franz Kafka* (2006)

Daniel Paul Schreber was a distinguished jurist who, shortly after being named President of the Court of Appeal of his region, had to be hospitalised with a paranoid delirious syndrome; his stay in the psychiatric hospital was to last seven years. Schreber undertook to write his *Memoirs of My Nervous Illness* (1903) as a plea for his release; the *Memoirs* owe their fame to Freud's analysis of them one year after their author's death.

Daniel Paul was the son of an educator who appears mad to us today, but who gained great fame in Germany at the end of the nineteenth century by writing numerous books on coercive and "orthopaedic" education. We know little about his mother, other than the fact that she held her illustrious husband in great esteem. At the age of forty-two, Daniel Paul was treated by Professor Flechsig for a "nervous breakdown".

111

He recovered, but nine years later, after a session of the *Land* Court of Appeal, he heard strange noises in the wall of his room and took them to be messages from God. The treatment—a sleep cure—which had proved successful the first time, remained without effect and the patient, in the midst of an end-of-the-world delirium, was transferred from Flechsig's clinic to the psychiatric hospital.

According to Schreber, the universal catastrophe he experienced a few days later was triggered by the temporary interruption of his wife's daily visits, when she had to go to Berlin to see her father. Suddenly, the world around Schreber was completely transformed. The city of Leipzig seemed destroyed, the sun far away, the world emptied of people or inhabited by "shadows of cursorily improvised men".

As for the inside of Schreber's body, it had become the site of transformations causing incredible suffering: for a while he had a destroyed lung and no intestines; one day he vomited his pharynx, another day his stomach was stolen and replaced with one that was inferior. While in the grip of these experiences, he told those who were looking after him that he suffered from a "loss of rays". Soon, negotiations with God were undertaken; the God in question had a double aspect (like in Zoroastrianism): a lower God, bent on destroying him, and an upper God whose role was to restore him. The alternate action of these two aspects of God was exercised in "a hedging system".

The most remarkable characteristic of the relation described by Schreber within this system is the total dependence in which God finds Himself vis-à-vis a creature—Schreber—to whom he has been tied by accident. Indeed, Schreber happens to be the one entrusted with the incredible task of maintaining the link between God and His creation. Schreber is fiercely determined to ward off God's "fading away" which would be a disaster for the world. This is why it is out of the question that he should think of nothing or that he should sleep. He is not granted the luxury of being able to say, like one of Georges Courteline's characters: "I rarely think, or when I do, I think of nothing." Schreber is not endowed with forgetting, and he cannot interrupt his psychic and sensory activity without fearing that God might fall out of the sky and that the world might disappear. He must stay on guard night and day, and can never relax his vigil.[1]

To describe the impossibility of interrupting the "forced thinking game", Schreber invents a scene we see as an excellent illustration of significant moments of his childhood. He asks his reader to imagine a situation where parents are present while their child is taking a school exam. Naturally, the parents will tend to answer for themselves the questions asked during the exam. But, in order to make it easier on their nerves and reduce the tension, they could turn their attention away from the exam and "focus it on a detail in their surroundings". This possibility open to the parents—focusing on something other than the test given the child—is not available to Schreber in relation to God.

We interpret the exam in this scene as referring to one of the sadistic tests Schreber's father used to inflict on him. And in the parent who needs to "make it easier on her nerves" and focus on an insignificant detail, we see a mother whose living portrait is best illustrated by incessantly cackling miraculous birds.[2] In this situation, Daniel Paul does not know what to do with himself.[3] Schreber comes back to the description of these talking birds again and again. Their insincere speech, resembling something learned by rote, is immediately recognisable by its tone and its rhythm; it differs from honest speech, which "attacks very quickly, with the rapid response characteristic of nervous reactions". By contrast, the rhythm of these memorised refrains is stretched out endlessly, and Schreber notes that the exaggerated slowness of the flow of these voices has always exasperated him to the point of distraction. The nerves of these birds have lost their natural ability to vibrate because they are coated with poison from corpses. Schreber attributes the putrid smell of death emanating from them to the human remains of beings selected in the "forecourts of heaven".

These "human remains" make us think of wounds, losses, secrets, and of crimes never prosecuted, kept quiet, and thereby prevented from existing before being forgotten. These crimes that have no psychic place of inscription because they were not represented in either thought or speech produce, several generations later, talking birds with an unnatural voice and an unbearable rhythm. Those of the first generation adapt, because "these things are not to be talked about", and because "life must go on". In the second and third generation there are guardians of the secret who see to it that nothing shows on the surface, but there are also individuals who kill themselves, have serious illnesses, or become drug addicts.

In the fourth generation there are talking birds that repeat phrases learned by heart and play out-of-tune instruments. These birds will not be content until the day they enter the child and partake in an orgasmic joy that they help bring about by doing him harm—like Kafka's vulture. When these talking birds start to spew ready-made phrases that they "utter without knowing the meaning of the words", the child, in his distress, perceives "a passing attack on the normal exercise of thinking". Taking advantage of the state of confusion they created, the birds enter the child and possess him.

For some parents, this is a way to evacuate the soul murder they carry unknowingly. Such a parent is not trying to kill the child, but is relieved to find in him a container in which to expel the monster he carries.[4] The means of this expulsion vary. Some people expel the monster by killing themselves, others transfer it into a spouse or a stranger, and often into a child. When a child is made into the depository of a silent but active memory, he automatically becomes, in spite of himself, an embarrassing witness. The troublesome witness of the murder of the witness. And try as he might, he does not understand why he feels so depressed.

Freud attempts to explain the onset of Schreber's illness by the hypothesis that a burst of homosexual libido triggered by overwork pushed the lawyer into developing a passion for his doctor, Professor Flechsig. Freud believes that the professor is the figure upon which Daniel Paul transfers the great love he still nurtures for his dead father and brother. This idea is not false in itself, but unfortunately it suggests the more surreptitious notion that the child carries an inherent mix of homosexuality and heterosexuality, the foundation of a "budding Oedipus"; and this foundation is presumed to develop depending on hereditary factors, life events, and accidents.

Thanks to men-from-the-country who have contributed to enriching the psychoanalytic field and widening its scope, we believe that during the sessions of the *Land* Court of Appeals, Schreber was confronted with the envy of some of his colleagues, and that he lost his head because he did not possess the warp yarn: hate, around which a coherent pattern could be woven.[5] In this situation, anyone with a protective shield on which the love-hate opposition could be inscribed, or from whom this opposition had not been erased, would have noticed the signs of hate and would have made sense of them. But Schreber did not dispose of such a protective device, and therefore did not perceive the murderous vibrations emitted by one or another of his colleagues. Soon, he came to feel isolated and could make no sense of his situation. The sentences spoken around him lost their meaning and his world became chaotic. In this scene, Schreber is paralysed and plunged into sensory deprivation, like the child in the hide-and-seek game played on the deserted city street. He finds himself in a situation that cannot resuscitate the memory of his childhood, but reproduces it nevertheless.

Schreber has no knowledge of hate, because both his parents transferred their hate into him innocently, unknowingly. All the signs that anyone else would be able to recognise are insignificant for him. He cannot see himself hated. He does not know what he swallowed because both his parents, accomplices in the commission of the crime, stuffed him, out of love, with the unnameable they passionately know nothing about.

Schreber loses his head not only because he is unable to perceive the hostile signs directed towards him, but also because the lack of encouragement from colleagues unconcerned with protecting his image plunges him into the abyss that has been his lot since early childhood. Not only is Schreber unable to name hostility and silence, he is unable to turn to his colleagues and ask for help. He cannot formulate a plea, he cannot ask for support. Schreber does not know that asking is possible. He has unlearned very early to ask for help. Turning to another, turning around, requires that the "I", the acting agency, be able to forget the ego, the guardian of continuity. For the child to be able to turn around, he has to have experienced a myriad of times that the other, the mother at first, is able to hold the memory of his dynamic displacement in his absence, so that she can find him not where she has left him, but where he has arrived. He has to have felt that the other carries his image during his absence, ensures his continuity while he is at play, in short, watches over him.

Schreber cannot see himself in the mirror his mother holds up to him. No image takes shape on the transitional matrix of this mother whose dreams are populated by incongruous shapes she cannot decipher. Schreber has to sustain an image of himself alone, and this is why he can never relax his vigil. He cannot let the mirror drop for a single moment lest the ego should collapse and the world be swept away. Like Narcissus, he cannot detach himself from his image because no one sees him. If Schreber should let himself think of nothing, he is quickly called back to order by foreshadowings of the end of the world that propel him out of his somnolence. When Schreber says that he cannot interrupt his thinking, he has to be taken literally. As soon as he interrupts the continuous game of reflection, he loses countenance and is threatened with becoming idiotic or losing vital organs. The image of his bodily ego is exposed to the risk of unthinkable devastation. His "I" cannot relinquish the responsibility of maintaining the persistence of his ego because there is no one else to assume this task.

Those to whom psychopathological nomenclature ascribes a "narcissistic personality" are those who had to maintain the image their parents failed to sustain, neglected for too long or neglected at a critical time. The so-called narcissistic personality corresponds to a situation where the "I" is in charge of the ego. As a result, the "I" can neither act nor relax its vigilance, and the ego complains to the "I" about being under constant surveillance.

The system of rays protects Schreber from annihilation. Out of the God who creates a miracle, who cannot do without him, who sends him wire-rays connected inside his skull, Schreber constructs a substitute psychic matrix. A system composed of God and his skull now ensures his psychosomatic balance and protects him from the return of the end of the world.

Freud conceived the theoretical corpus of psychoanalysis from the subjective position of a person endowed with an original paradoxical system made up of an *I* and an *ego*. He presumed the presence of the paradoxical entity of self-reflection that testifies to the unconditional "seduction-restraint" of which the child was the object. Freud did not imagine the possibility that such a paradoxical system could be absent. This is why he could not sympathise with Schreber: he interpreted his transformation into a woman as a primary, ontological phenomenon that resurfaced after having been repressed, or incompletely repressed, which amounts to the same thing. Freud confuses a wish-fulfilment fantasy with a means of survival.

In truth, Schreber invents a site from which he can be seen. Because he was not seen in the mirror of a parental dream, Schreber invents a place from which he is seen. This hallucination is not a product of the economy of desire, but of the need to exist. Since such a person has not met another who performs this function, he takes on the function the other should perform. In Schreber's case this other is God, but, in general, it could just as well be a neighbour who sees you and talks to you. Most often, the neighbour does not wish you well, but at least he wishes you something. In the normal subject—according to Lacan, the subject of the unconscious is divided—the two agencies (the I and the ego) are indissociable and the person can choose one position or the other depending on whether he wants to act, think, or rest. The paradoxical system constructed by Schreber is a vicarious system. The one who says "I" and the one who watches him and talks to him, God—but a God dependent on the "I"—form an inseparable pair that will substitute itself to the I–me pair that Schreber did not have the opportunity to constitute.

Schreber's "he hates me" is created *ex nihilo* and protects him from the void. Schreber has recourse to hate to compensate for his mother's withdrawal. To compensate for the absence of an image in the mirror held out to him by his mother and by the illustrious professor who had been his miraculous healer nine years earlier,[6] Schreber sets in place the will to destroy. He replaces "He does not see me" with "He can't stand to see me", which gives him an image in the mirror because it shows that "someone" reacts to him. Since he cannot be an object of love, he escapes indifference by setting up hate, a hate he has to nurture and to bear.

Schreber was *"de-tested"*, meaning that the testimony of his senses was denied. His parents worked at killing the witness in him and passed their crime off as a pedagogical procedure. Erasing the harm they inflict in this manner is the crime of negationist parents.[7] The first effect of this denial of justice is to create in the child a naivety that blinds him to any harm about to be inflicted on him. Schreber "does not see evil", and this is the first benign sign of his problems of judgment. Paradoxically, he has no way of perceiving the hostile vibrations occasionally emitted by his friends and those who wish him well. He is not equipped to recognise them and deal with them. Signs of hate sent in his direction find no recipient and leave him destroyed on the spot, like the American fleet at Pearl Harbor, because surveillance radars had not picked up any signals. In Schreber's case, objective, external hate has no subjective, internal support. As a result, his image faces a highly alarming scenario. Instantly, he loses countenance and is banished from reality. He is no longer participating in an exchange with someone else, he is radically alone, more alone than a speleologist in a prolonged state of sensory deprivation. In a short time, hallucinatory effects appear: his body image dissolves and his internal organs feel strange to him.

Because Schreber was de-tested of the hate directed against him, he is deprived of the inscription of this emotion on his psychic matrix; when an unexpected attack takes place—and the attack is always unexpected—this deprivation causes the breakdown of the subject. To counter this catastrophic occurrence, the subject improvises in a panic a system in which he is the object of hate. He invents a persecutor. But the hate he attributes to an individual chosen among his friends and protectors is not a reproduction of the erased hate whose object he once was, but rather something created on the site of an erasure. As a result, this hate is indestructible and cannot be attenuated by an external other, since it does not depend on him. Deprived of a love-hate paradoxical system, Schreber invents a protector who hates him. This does not allow him to see himself in the mirror, but his image now depends on the one to whom he attributes this out of the ordinary hate. The consistency of his image depends on the hate he attributes to Flechsig; for this reason, he cannot turn his back on his miracle worker, and cannot separate from him.

When Freud wrote to Karl Abraham that he succeeded where the paranoiac fails, he meant that he was able to turn his back on his own miracle worker and confidant. He is able to do so because his image of himself is not entirely dependent on his friend and colleague. Freud does not depend on Fliess to see himself because he inherited a consistent image. Like every normal child, he had a parent able to testify to his own affect when he felt hate for the child. By attesting to his emotions, even the most undesirable ones, this parent was giving the child a coherent image of his ego.[8] Thus, hate could become, in this child, a solid weft for the weave. He was often able to find support in this sensation and tie it to an event or to the languages of the mother who testified to it. Under these conditions, hate could uphold his experience. Later, when hate appears in his relationship with a friend, specifically Fliess, he is neither surprised nor at a loss. He can repress its signs because he "knows" them. At the right moment, he will be able to read them, translate them, and bring them into play in favourable circumstances. His parents have given him the gift of an image able to withstand, if not absolutely anything, at least the test of hate (Derrida, 1992a).[9] The protective shield of a normal child comprises the duality love-hate and confers consistency and independence to the image of the ego.

Schreber's hate for Flechsig could diminish once Schreber acquired a vicarious paradox able to endow him with an image of the ego that can replace the image which was destroyed. Little by little, Schreber builds a paradoxical system in which the oxymoron (or paradoxicality) is the key element. The inner language the jurist invents at the beginning of his stay in the asylum is replete with such oxymorons. For example, *miracle* stands for *torture*, *reward* stands for *punishment*, *poison* for *food*, and *impiety* for *saint*. But this language extended to all his vital functions, creating a situation which obliterated his ability to act, so much so that his doctor, Dr Weber, writes in his report appended to the *Memoirs* that his patient "… remained immobile, lying down or standing, and refused nourishment of any sort, so that he had to be forcibly fed." The same contradiction, inherent in the *inner language*, makes Schreber postpone his bowel movements as long as possible. A few months later, when the rhetorical system came to spare vital functions like eating, sleeping, evacuation, and breathing, in order to maintain the opposition Schreber invented the support given by *divine miracles* in the form of sensory torture. Later, these miracles diminished and were replaced by the major oxymoron of being transformed into a woman, a configuration in which his psychotic system stabilised. With this transformation into a sex which is "his" because it is not his, Schreber succeeded, as well as he could, in resexualising his world and in giving himself a new ego.

By changing his image, Schreber created a new subject. At the end of this process of creation, the Subject Schreber, transformed, has become viable. He has given himself a stable ego image. In the process, he has constructed a vicarious paradoxical system. He has passed through otherness, the image of the woman, to come out of the confusion in which his mother and father had left him. In this way, Schreber reached the shores of humanity where differences are acknowledged and where each thing is distinct from every other thing. Between his masculine first name and the feminine image of his body there is now a stable opposition that compensates for "in-difference".[10]

Schreber's healing is catastrophic. To oppose the unnameable thing that was transposed into him, to offer opposition to the destruction of the paradoxical system that took place during this transposition, Schreber invented a solution: he discovered unmanning, *Entmannung*. He gave his ego a status against which the destructive rays were powerless.

> Until then, I still considered it possible that … it would eventually be necessary for me to end it by suicide … But now I could see beyond doubt that the Order of the World imperiously demanded my unmanning … and that therefore it was common sense that nothing was left to me but to reconcile myself to the thought of being transformed into a woman. (p. 164)

> I would like to meet the man who, faced with the choice of either becoming a demented human being in male habitus or a spirited woman, would not prefer the latter. Such and only such is the issue for me. (pp. 164–165)

As soon as he is transformed into a woman, suicide is no longer the only means Schreber has for finding his place in life. Through the sacrifice of his genetic and psychic sexual identity, accomplished in extremely painful conditions, Schreber recovers a faculty of perception that allows him to participate in common sense. Thanks to this feat through which he constructs a vicarious paradoxical system, he is able to perceive the same images and sounds as other human beings, and can dispense with mediation through a persecutor. Not having received from his parents the gift of an image, Schreber constructed a vicarious paradox he could use as support.

Notes

1. In the circumstances contrary to the order of the world which have now arisen this relation has changed—and I wish to mention this at the outset—the weather is now to a certain extent dependent on *my* actions and thoughts; as soon as I indulge in thinking nothing, […] the wind arises at once. (Schreber, 1903, p. 22).

   But as soon as I turn my gaze or allow my eyes to be closed by miracles, or as soon as I change from talking aloud to silence without at the same time starting some mental occupation, in other words when I give myself up to thinking nothing, the following phenomena which are interrelated occur almost at once:

   > Noises around me, …
   > In my own person the advent of the bellowing miracle …
   > The winds arise, …
   > The cries of "help" […] of god's nerves …

   (ibid., p. 188).

2. The miraculously created birds […] have not the least understanding of what they have spoken before, i.e. for the phrases learnt by rote [… their] nerves being made *immune* against all sensation which they would otherwise have entering my body, […] just as if they entered

into me blindfolded or with their natural capacity for feeling somehow suspended. (ibid., p. 192).

[These birds] completely lost the capacity to think and apparently only retained that degree of sensibility which allows them to appreciate or enjoy sharing the voluptuousness which they meet in my body. (ibid., p. 285).

3. Altogether I was not allowed to remain for long in one and the same position or at the same occupation: when I was walking one attempted to force me to lie down, and when I was lying down one wanted to chase me off my bed. Rays did not seem to appreciate that a human being who actually exists *must be somewhere*. Because of the irresistible attraction of my nerves I had become an embarrassing human being for the rays (for God). [...] One did not want to admit that what had happened was not my fault, but one always tended to reverse the blame by way of "representing". (ibid., p. 151).

4. Their property as erstwhile human nerves is evidenced by the fact that *all* the miraculously produced birds *without exception*, whenever they have completely unloaded the poison of corpses which they carry, that is to say when they have reeled off the phrases drummed into them, then express *in human sounds the genuine* feeling of well being in the soul-voluptuousness of my body which they share, with the words "damned fellow" or "somehow damned", *the only words in which they are still capable of giving expression to genuine feeling*. (ibid., p. 191. The emphasis throughout is Schreber's).

5. The task (presiding over the Superior Court of Dresden) was all the heavier [... as] the members of the panel of five judges over which I had to preside ... almost all of them were much senior to me (up to twenty years), and anyway they were much more intimately acquainted with the procedure of the court, to which I was a newcomer. (ibid., p. 47).

6. [...] Professor Flechsig developed a remarkable eloquence which affected me deeply. He spoke of the advances made in psychiatry since my first illness, of newly discovered sleeping drugs, etc., and gave me hope that the whole illness, through one prolific sleep ... (p. 48).

Here the verb is missing and the sentence remains unfinished. This truncated utterance, the only one of its kind in the book, recalls the chopped-off phrases of the talking birds.

7. Analysands often defend their parents, saying that the negation was "unconscious". Whether it was conscious or not could no doubt interest a judge who has to determine whether there are extenuating circumstances, but does not interest the psychoanalyst, for whom this negation is an act.

8. Such a mother can hate the child, and she sometimes does, but she never de-tests him. See endnote 42.

9. In his book *Given Time* (1992b), Jacques Derrida speaks of the contradictory nature of the gift and shows that there can only be a gift if neither the giver nor the receiver see it as such. A gift can only exist on condition that it remains unknown. Derrida adds that in order to speak of it, we would have to invent a terminology which is neither philosophical nor psychoanalytic. In our opinion, the giving of a psychic apparatus is the only gift possible, since it is the only act that combines memory and forgetting. The psychic apparatus symbolises the paradox: in Nicolas Abraham's terms, this means that one of the elements of opposition is forgotten. The representation of the thing which corresponds to death is absent from the unconscious. In place of the representation of a thing stands the ability to represent oneself. Unlike Derrida, I would not say that the psychic apparatus represents death, but rather that it is the paradox life-and-death transformed into a function. It illustrates the leap taken above impossible indifference, indivisibility, indecision.

10. The mother who has no internal image of her child only sees him from the outside, like everyone else does; as a result, the child is forced to sustain his own image, to give himself the negative—an exhausting task and, above all, a task impossible to accomplish at the moment when the subject has to become aware of his reflection. In order to act, the subject must have an image independent of himself. Without this support, he cannot make a choice and come out of indecision. When he finds himself in this situation, he either breaks the spell or enters a crisis from which he might emerge like Schreber: having forged a new subject, a paradoxical entity, I–me.

REFERENCES

Abraham, N., & Torok, M. (1994). *The Shell and the Kernel*. Chicago, IL: University of Chicago Press.

Benveniste, E. (1966 & 1974). *Problems in General Linguistics, Vols. 1 & 2*. Miami, FL: University of Miami Press.

Bion, W. R. (1967). *Second Thoughts* (p. 104). London: William Heinemann Medical.

Blanchot, M. (1992). *The Step Not Beyond* (p. 48). Albany, NJ: State University of New York Press.

Cacciari, M. (1990). *Les Icônes de la Loi*. Paris: Christian Bourgois.

Char, R. (1966). Encart. In: *Le Nu Perdu et autres poèmes*. Paris: Gallimard.

Citati, P. (1990). Une année dans la vie de Franz Kafka. In: *Franz Kafka, Lettres à ses parents*. Paris: Gallimard.

Davoine, F. (2012). *Wittgenstein's Folly*. New York: PYBK.

Delaunay, P. (1989). Dimensions dites "psychotiques" des transferts. In: *Correspondances Freudiennes, No 26*. Lyon, France: Fédération des Ateliers de Psychanalyse.

Derrida, J. (1978). Freud and the scene of writing. In: *Writing and Difference* (p. 224 ff.). Chicago, IL: University of Chicago Press.

Derrida, J. (1992a). *On the Name*. Cambridge: Cambridge University Press.

Derrida, J. (1992b). *Given Time*. Chicago, IL: University of Chicago Press.

Ferenczi, S. (1949). Confusion of tongues between adult and child. *International Journal of Psychoanalysis, 30*: 225–230.

Ferenczi, S. (1988). Clinical diary. *Blackwell Synergy—Journal of Analytical Psychology, 48*(4): 479–489.

Fliess, W. (1906). *Der Ablauf des Lebens* (*The Course of Life*) (p. 252 ff.) Leipzig, Germany: F. Deuticke.

Fliess, W. (1909). *Vom Leben und vom Tod* (*About Life and Death*). Jena, Germany: Eugen Dieterich.

Freud, S. (1900a). *The Interpretation of Dreams. S. E., 4, 5*. London: Hogarth.

Freud, S. (1910c). *Leonardo da Vinci and a Memory of his Childhood. S. E., 11.* London: Hogarth.

Freud, S. (1912–13). *Totem and Taboo. S. E., 13*. London: Hogarth.

Freud, S. (1914c). On narcissism: An introduction. *S. E., 14*: 75. London: Hogarth.

Freud, S. (1915d). Repression. *S. E., 14*: 159–204. London: Hogarth.

Freud, S. (1917d). A metapsychological supplement to the theory of dreams. *S. E., 14*: 237–258. London: Hogarth.

Freud, S. (1920g). *Beyond the Pleasure Principle. S. E., 18*. London: Hogarth.

Freud, S. (1925a). A note upon the "Mystic Writing-Pad". *S. E., 19*: 227–234. London: Hogarth.

Freud, S. (1925h). *Negation. S. E., 19*: 235–239. London: Hogarth.

Freud, S. (1950a). A project for a scientific psychology. *S. E., 1*. London: Hogarth.

Freud, S. (2002). *The Schreber Case*. A. Webber (Trans.). London: Penguin Classics.

Goux, J. -J. (1990). *Oedipe Philosophe*. Paris: Aubier.

Hölderlin, J. C. F. (1803). Remarks on Oedipus. In: Essays and Letters on Theory (T. Pfau, Trans.). Albany, NY: State University of New York Press, 1988.

Hölderlin, J. C. F. (1804). *Remarks on the Translation of Sophocles*. Stuttgart, Germany: Metzler, 1961.

Jarszyk, G. (1999). *Le Négatif ou l'Ecriture de l'Autre dans la Logique de Hegel* (p. 239). Paris: Ellipses.

Jung, C. G. (1963). *Memories, Dreams and Reflections* (p. 157). London: Collins and Routledge & Kegan Paul.

Kafka, F. (1910). Meditations on sin, suffering, hope and the true path. Cologne, Germany: Kiepenheuer & Witsch, 1931.

Kafka, F. (1913). The judgment. In: N. N. Glatzer (Ed.), *The Complete Stories of Franz Kafka*. New York: Schocken, 1971.

Kafka, F. (1915). *The Metamorphosis*. New York: Bantam Classics, 1972.

Kafka, F. (1916). Before the law. In: N. N. Glatzer (Ed.), *The Complete Stories of Franz Kafka*. New York: Schocken, 1971.

Kafka, F. (1917). The third notebook. In: M. Brod (Ed.), E. Kaiser & E. Wilkins (Trans.), *The Blue Octavo Notebooks*. Cambridge, MA: Exact Change, 1971.

Kafka, F. (1919). Up in the gallery. In: N. N. Glatzer (Ed.), *The Complete Stories of Franz Kafka*. New York: Schocken, 1971.

Kafka, F. (1924). Josephine the Singer, or the Mouse Folk. In: N. N. Glatzer (Ed.), *The Complete Stories of Franz Kafka*. New York: Schocken, 1971.

Kafka, F. (1931a). The bridge. In: N. N. Glatzer (Ed.), *The Complete Stories of Franz Kafka*. New York: Schocken, 1971.

Kafka, F. (1931b). Prometheus. In: N. N. Glatzer (Ed.), *The Complete Stories of Franz Kafka*. New York: Schocken, 1971.

Kafka, F. (1931c). The silence of the Sirens. In: N. N. Glatzer (Ed.), *The Complete Stories of Franz Kafka*. New York: Schocken, 1971.

Kafka, F. (1936a). The vulture. In: N. N. Glatzer (Ed.), *The Complete Stories of Franz Kafka*. New York: Schocken, 1971.

Kafka, F. (1936b). The test. In: N. N. Glatzer (Ed.), *The Complete Stories of Franz Kafka*. New York: Schocken, 1971.

Kafka, F. (1948). *The Kafka Diaries*: 1910–1923 (p. 129). New York: Schocken, 1976.

Kafka, F. (2006). *The Zürau Aphorisms of Franz Kafka*. (R. Calasso, Ed.; M. Hofmann, Trans.). New York: Schocken.

Lacoue-Labarthe, P. (1987). *La Fiction du Politique* (pp. 64–72). Paris: Christian Bourgois.

Levinas, E. (1993). *God, Death and Time*. Stanford, NJ: Stanford University Press.

Lindon, J. (1990). *Jonas*. Paris: Les Editions de Minuit.

Lyotard, J. -F. (1971). Le non et la position de l'objet. In: *Discourse, Figure* (p. 117 ff.). Paris: Klinicksieck.

Masson, J. M. (Ed.) (1985). *The Complete Letters of Sigmund Freud to Wilhelm Fliess, 1887–1904* (p. 15). Cambridge, MA: Harvard University Press.

Merleau-Ponty, M. (1964). *Eye and Mind*. J. E. Edie (Ed.). Evanston, IL: Northwestern University Press.

Proust, M. (1918). *Within a Budding Grove. Remembrance of Things Past, Vol. II*. London: Vintage, 1981.

Proust, M. (1923). *The Prisoner. Remembrance of Things Past, Vol. V*. London: Vintage, 1981.

Rilke, R. M. (1898). *The Book of Hours*. A. Barrows (Trans.). New York: Riverhead, 1997.

Rilke, R. M. (1903). The book of poverty and death. In: A. Barrows (Trans.), *The Book of Hours*. New York: Riverhead, 1997.

Rilke, R. M. (1922). *Sonnets to Orpheus* (p. 71). New York: The Norton Library, 1962.

Robert, M. (2012). *Introduction à la lecture de Kafka*. Paris: Editions de l'Eclat.

Schaffer, E. S. (Ed.) (1983). The meaning of tragedies. In: *Comparative criticism. A Yearbook, Vol. 5*. Cambridge: Cambridge University Press.

Schreber, D. P. (1903). *Memoirs of My Nervous Illness*. New York: Macmillan, 2000.

Searles, H. F. (Ed.) (1970). *Countertransference and Related Subjects*. New York: International Universities Press, 1979.

Sloterdijk, P. (1997). *Critique of Cynical Reason*. Minneapolis, MN: University of Minnesota Press.

Sophocles. *Philoctetes* (p. 253 ff.). Cambridge, MA: Loeb Classical Library, Harvard University Press, 1994.

Staal, F. (Ed.) (1983). *Agni: The Vedic Ritual of the Fire Altar*. Delhi, India: Motilal Banarsidass, 2002.

Thom, R. (1975). *Catastrophe Theory: Its Present State and Future Perspectives*. Berlin: Springer.

Uexküll, J. V. (2010). *Foray into the Worlds of Animals and Humans*. Minneapolis, MN: University of Minnesota Press.

Verlet, L. (1993). *La malle de Newton*. Paris: Gallimard,

Winnicott, D. W. (1971). *Playing and Reality* (p. 12). London: Tavistock.

Wittgenstein, L. (1968). *The Philosophical Investigations: Section 50*. London: Macmillan.

Wittgenstein, L. (1978). *Philosophical Remarks*. London: Blackwell.

INDEX

127